spice of life

spice of life

50 aromatic recipes to tantalize your tastebuds

consulting editor sophy friend

southwater

This edition is published by Southwater

Distributed in the UK by
The Manning Partnership
251–253 London Road East
Batheaston
Bath BA1 7RL
tel. 01225 852 727
fax 01225 852 852

Published in the USA by
Anness Publishing Inc.
27 West 20th Street
Suite 504
New York
NY 10011
fax 212 807 6813

Distributed in Canada by
General Publishing
895 Don Mills Road
400–402 Park Centre
Toronto, Ontario M3C 1W3
tel. 416 445 3333
fax 416 445 5991

Distributed in Australia by
Sandstone Publishing
Unit 1, 360 Norton Street
Leichhardt
New South Wales 2040
tel. 02 9560 7888
fax 02 9560 7488

Southwater is an imprint of Anness Publishing Limited
Hermes House, 88–89 Blackfriars Road, London SE1 8HA
tel. 020 7401 2077; fax 020 7633 9499

© 1998, 2001 Anness Publishing Limited

Publisher: Joanna Lorenz
Consultant Editor: Sophy Friend
Designer: Brian Weldon
Indexer: Dorothy Frame
Jacket design: The Bridgewater Book Company Limited
Photographer: William Adams-Lingwood, Edward Allright, David Armstrong,
Steve Baxter, James Duncan, Michelle Garrett, Amanda Heywood, David Jordan,
Thomas Odulate, Peter Reilly
Recipes: Catherine Atkinson, Sarah Edmonds, Silvana Franco, Sarah Gates, Shirley Gill,
Elisabeth Lambert Ortiz, Shehzad Husain, Manisha Kanani, Ruby Le Bois, Sue Maggs,
Annie Nichols, Jenny Stacey, Liz Trigg, Steven Wheeler
Production Controller: Joanna King

Notes

For all recipes, quantities are given in both metric and imperial measures and, where
appropriate, measures are also given in standard cups and spoons. Follow one set, but not
a mixture, because they are not interchangeable.

Standard spoon and cup measures are level.
1 tsp = 5ml, 1 tbsp = 15ml, 1 cup = 250ml/8fl oz

Australian standard tablespoons are 20ml. Australian readers should use 3 tsp in place of
1 tbsp for measuring small quantities of gelatine, cornflour, salt, etc.

Medium eggs are used unless otherwise stated.

Previously published as *Step-by-Step: Cooking with Spices*

1 3 5 7 9 10 8 6 4 2

CONTENTS

INTRODUCTION

Variety, as the old proverb says, is the spice of life – and, in culinary terms, the dazzling array and variety of spices we have at our fingertips add a wealth of colour, richness and flavour to food.

Today, in most large supermarkets, we are able to buy ready-prepared curry powders, chillies and spice pastes in jars and cans that are of excellent quality, reflecting our increasing interest in spicy foods. However, for more subtle combinations, it is worth experimenting by making up your own mixtures.

Almost every country in the world has its own individual and distinctive way of spicing up its food, from the ever-popular curries of India, fiery hot chilli-laden dishes of Mexico, hot and sour dishes of Thailand and zesty recipes of Africa to a smattering of unexpectedly spicy favourites from Europe.

You will find some classic spicy dishes in this book such as Beef Vindaloo, Thai Pork Satay and Gingercake as well as some delicious new ideas like Blackened Redfish, Pumpkin and Pistachio Risotto with Saffron and Crispy Cinnamon Toasts.

Whether you choose to create an entire menu of spicy dishes – or just whizz up a spicy snack – this cookbook is sure to spice up your life.

Spices and Seasonings

Spices come in a variety of different forms, from fresh to dried and ground. These are some of the most frequently used spices in this cookbook.

Allspice
This is available in both whole and ground forms and imparts a flavouring that is similar to a mixture of nutmeg, cinnamon, cloves and pepper.

Caraway Seeds
A pungent and aromatic spice, which is widely used in German and Austrian cooking. The seeds are often scattered over breads and small rolls before baking.

Cardamom Pods
Cardamom pods are usually green. They should be broken open and the small black seeds ground to fully develop the mellow, fragrant, slightly spicy aroma.

Cayenne Pepper
Ground from small red chillies, this is extremely spicy and should be used with caution. It is very popular in Indian and Mexican cooking.

Cinnamon
Cinnamon is a sweet and fragrant spice ground from the dried, rolled inner bark of a tropical tree that is native to Sri Lanka.

Cloves
A strongly aromatic spice with a slightly bitter taste, most frequently used in sweet dishes and mulled drinks.

Coriander
A sweet, warm aromatic spice that is used widely in Indian and South-east Asian cooking.

Cumin
A uniquely flavoured spice with a sweetly pungent and very distinctive taste. It is widely used in Middle-eastern cooking.

Fennel Seeds
These seeds have a strong, sweet anise-liquorice flavour. They are particularly good to use in fish dishes.

Nutmeg
A very aromatic spice with a warm, sweet, nutty flavour. Often used in milk puddings.

Paprika
The flavour can range from sweet and lightly piquant, to pungent and fiery. It is an important ingredient in Hungarian goulashes.

Star Anise
A sweet, pungent liquorice-flavoured spice, which is particularly important in Chinese cooking. It is the dominant flavour in Chinese five spice powder. It is also used in some alcoholic drinks and confectionery.

Ginger
The fresh root has a clean, refreshing, slightly sharp flavour. Ginger is also available dried and ground. It can be used in sweet dishes such as gingercake, and savoury dishes such as pickles and chutneys.

Lemon Grass
A strong, refreshing citrus flavouring which is frequently used in many dishes in Thai and Vietnamese cooking.

Juniper Berries
These pine-scented, bittersweet berries provide gin with its distinctive flavour. They are used in game bird dishes, pork, lamb, and ham. They are also excellent when used to flavour meat pâtés and terrines.

Saffron
This is the most expensive spice in the world, taken from crocus flowers. You only need a small amount to flavour and colour any dish. It is used in rice dishes in India, Spain and Italy.

Turmeric
Mainly used for its bright yellow colouring, it can be used as an inexpensive substitute for saffron. It has a slightly musky aroma. Turmeric is an essential spice in curries and is also used in chutneys and pickles.

Yellow Mustard Seeds
These seeds are less pungent than brown or black mustard seeds. They have a sweet, mild piquancy. The most common use for these seeds is to drop them into a vinegar solution when pickling vegetables.

Useful Equipment for Preparing Spices

Spices are often ground, crushed, pounded or puréed to create powders and pastes. These items of equipment make the tasks much easier.

Nutmeg Graters
These come in a variety of sizes. They have very small rough holes and produce a fine powder. The one on the left doubles as a storage container.

Garlic Press
A simple garlic press makes quick and easy work of crushing garlic cloves.

China Pestle and Mortar
Smooth china pestles and mortars come in many sizes and are excellent for grinding small amounts of dry spices.

Granite Pestle and Mortar
Traditional Indian and Oriental granite or stone pestles and mortars are generally fairly large, with deep, pitted or ridged bowls and heavy pestles. They are ideal for pounding fresh spices, such as ginger, galangal and lemon grass, as the rough surface seems to grip the pieces and prevents them flying out of the bowl while you pound the mixture.

Bowl-shaped Pestle and Mortar
Bigger, flat-bowled pestles and mortars are particularly good for making spice pastes that include large amounts of fresh spices, herbs, onion and garlic.

Nutmeg Mill
Nutmeg mills work by rotating the nutmeg over a blade – different models grate with varying degrees of success.

Electric Coffee Grinder
An electric coffee grinder is excellent for grinding dry spices. If you are going to do a lot of spice cooking, it is worth keeping a separate grinder purely for this purpose.

Perspex Mill
This small clear perspex mill can be used to grind both cinnamon and cassia bark.

Electric Food Processor
Electric food processors are invaluable for making large quantities of spice pastes.

Ginger Grater
Traditional wooden Japanese ginger graters make it easy to grate ginger, and they are easy to clean. A stainless steel box grater also works well. Use the finest grating surface and work over a plate to catch the juices.

Preparing Lemon Grass

Use the whole stem and remove it before serving or chop it finely.

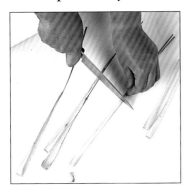 

1 Lay the lemon grass on a chopping board. Using a sharp knife, cut off the woody parts from the top and bottom.

2 Cut across the lemon grass stalks to make thin slices, then continue chopping until fine.

Preparing Chillies

Chillies add a distinctive flavour, but remove the seeds as they are fiery hot.

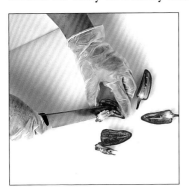 

1 Wearing rubber gloves, remove the stalks from the chillies. Then cut the chillies in half lengthways. Using a small sharp knife, scrape out the seeds and fleshy white ribs from each half.

2 Cut the chillies into thin slices lengthways, then cut across to make fine dice.

Preparing Garlic with a Garlic Press

One of the quickest and cleanest ways to prepare garlic is to use a metal or plastic garlic press.

1 Using a garlic press, leave the clove unpeeled and cut off the root end. Place the clove cut end down in the press.

2 Crush the clove into a bowl. The garlic skin can be removed in one piece, making the press easier to clean.

Preparing Garlic without a Garlic Press

If you don't own a garlic press: try this method, which gives wonderful juicy results.

1 Peel the outer papery layer off the garlic bulb. Cut the ends off the cloves.

2 Crush the cloves flat to extract all of the juices. Then chop finely.

Grating Whole Nutmeg and Fresh Ginger

An excellent way to prepare nutmeg and root ginger for cooking.

1 To get a fine powder of nutmeg, use a specialized nutmeg grater. Place the grater on a board, then simply rub the whole nutmeg against the grater.

2 To grate ginger, peel the root, then grate it on the fine blade of a stainless steel grater until you have the amount you require.

Preparing Kaffir Lime Leaves

Kaffir lime leaves have a strong flavour and are best shredded for recipes.

1 Roll the kaffir lime leaves into cigar shapes, then shred them finely.

2 If the leaves are old, cut out the central stalk before shredding.

Preparing Fresh Ginger and Turmeric

Fresh root ginger and turmeric roots can be used in slices, strips or finely chopped.

1 Peel the skin from the root ginger, then using a cleaver or a chef's knife, cut it into thin slices.

2 To cut ginger into shreds, arrange the slices one on top of another, cut lengthways into strips, then chop finely.

3 Peel turmeric in the same way as ginger. The bright colour will stain heavily, so it is a good idea to wear rubber gloves. Once peeled, the fresh turmeric can be sliced, chopped or ground to a paste with other ingredients. It can be cooked in the same way as fresh root ginger.

How to Store Spices

Very few cooks store their spices in the correct way. Dried spices are usually displayed in clear glass jars on the kitchen shelf or in wall-mounted spice racks, and fresh spices, such as root ginger or lemon grass, are often just kept on a kitchen shelf or in a vegetable rack. Here are some tips on how to preserve the flavour and aroma of your spices.

Storing Fresh Spices

Unless you are going to use fresh spices on the day they are bought, they should be chilled rather than stored at room temperature. Lemon grass, kaffir lime leaves and curry leaves are best wrapped in a piece of kitchen paper and stored in the salad drawer of a fridge for up to 2 weeks. Fresh galangal, root ginger and chillies will keep for up to 3 weeks in a sealed container, lined with kitchen paper, in the fridge. If you would like to keep them longer, fresh spices can be pounded to a paste, then put in small sealed containers and frozen for up to 6 months.

Storing Dried Spices

Both ground and whole dried spices should be stored in airtight containers in a cool, dark cupboard or drawer as light, heat and moisture lessen their quality. Whole spices will keep for 6 months or even longer, if stored carefully. However, most ground spices lose their colour, flavour and aroma within 5 or 6 months. If you are unsure just how long the spices have been stored, check the aroma – if the spice smells musty, or if there is little aroma, it is likely that the flavour will be impaired, too. It's a good idea to label new jars of spices with the date of purchase.

Storing Other Spices

Bottles or tubes of spice pastes and purées, such as ginger or garlic purée, will keep unopened until the best-before date. However, once opened, they should be stored in the fridge and used within 6 weeks. Both dried and ready-made mustard will keep for up to a year even

Small glass jars with airtight seals or screw tops are perfectly good containers for storing dried spices, providing they are kept in a cool dark cupboard. Avoid displaying them on a rack on the wall, or on a kitchen shelf as their flavours will deteriorate.

when opened. Dried tamarind and vanilla pods will keep in a cool dark place for up to 2 years.

Opaque jars made of either china or metal don't need to be stored in a dark place, but they are still better kept in a cool cupboard out of the heat of the kitchen.

This stainless steel spice container is ideal for storing dried spices. The individual pots are sealed when the inner lid is closed: a second lid ensures that no light or moisture gets into the tin.

POWDERS AND PASTES

Curry Powder

Curry powders are a combination of the particular spices of an area.

Makes about 250 ml/8 fl oz/1 cup

INGREDIENTS

6-8 dried red chillies
120 ml/4 fl oz/½ cup coriander seeds
60 ml/4 tbsp cumin seeds
10 ml/2 tsp fenugreek seeds
10 ml/2 tsp black mustard seeds
10 ml/2 tsp black peppercorns
15 ml/1 tbsp ground turmeric
5 ml/1 tsp ground ginger

1 Remove the stalks and seeds from the chillies, unless you like a fiery mixture, in which case leave a few seeds in the pods.

2 Roast or dry-fry the chillies, coriander, cumin, fenugreek, mustard seeds and black peppercorns in a dry heavy-based pan over a medium heat until they begin to brown and give off a rich aroma. Shake the pan frequently so that the spices are evenly roasted.

3 Grind the roasted spices to a powder in a mortar or coffee grinder, then stir in the turmeric and ginger.

cumin seeds

ground turmeric

dried red chillies

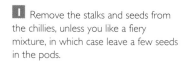
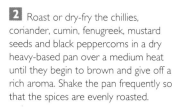

coriander seeds

Sambaar Powder

This classic blend of spices is used extensively in South Indian dishes to flavour vegetable and lentil combinations, braised dishes and spicy broths.

Makes about 250 ml/8 fl oz/1 cup

INGREDIENTS

8-10 dried red chillies
90 ml/6 tbsp coriander seeds
30 ml/2 tbsp cumin seeds
10 ml/2 tsp black peppercorns
10 ml/2 tsp fenugreek seeds
10 ml/2 tsp urad dhal or white split gram beans
10 ml/2 tsp chana dhal or yellow split peas
10 ml/2 tsp mung dhal or yellow mung beans
25 ml/1½ tbsp ground turmeric

1 Discard the stalks and seeds from the chillies. Heat a dry heavy-based frying pan, add the chillies, coriander, cumin, black peppercorns and fenugreek. Toss all the spices together over a medium heat until they give off a rich aroma, then turn the mixture into a bowl.

2 Repeat the process with the pulses, tossing them over a medium heat continuously until they are toasted, but do not allow them to burn.

3 Grind the spices and pulses to a fine powder and then mix in the turmeric.

fenugreek seeds

mung dhal

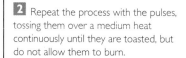

chana dhal

dried red chillies

Garam Masala

Garam means warm or hot, and masala means spices. This is a North Indian spice mix.

Makes about 250 ml/8 fl oz/1 cup

INGREDIENTS

10 green cardamom pods
90 ml/6 tbsp coriander seeds
60 ml/4 tbsp cumin seeds
10 cloves
5 cm/2 in piece cinnamon stick
15 ml/1 tbsp black peppercorns
3 dried bay leaves
15 ml/1 tbsp ground mace

1 Gently warm a dry heavy-based pan before adding the spices.

2 Bruise the cardamom pods and place them in the pan with the coriander, cumin, cloves, cinnamon stick, peppercorns and bay leaves. Keep tossing the spices over a gentle heat until they give off a rich aroma.

3 Remove the seeds from the cardamoms and break the cinnamon stick into small pieces. Grind all the spices to a fine powder, then mix in the ground mace.

cumin seeds

cloves

bay leaves

Kashmiri Masala

This masala is particularly good with prawn and lamb dishes.

Makes 90 ml/6 tbsp

INGREDIENTS

12 green cardamom pods
5 cm/2 in piece cinnamon stick
15 ml/1 tbsp cloves
15 ml/1 tbsp black peppercorns
15 ml/1 tbsp black cumin seeds
10 ml/2 tsp caraway seeds
5 ml/1 tsp freshly grated nutmeg

cinnamon stick

grated nutmeg

green cardamom pods

1 Split the cardamom pods and break the cinnamon stick into pieces.

2 Warm a dry heavy-based frying pan and then dry-fry all the spices except the nutmeg, tossing them continuously, until they give off a rich aroma.

3 Remove the cardamom seeds from their pods and grind all the spices to a fine powder. Mix in the nutmeg.

Chat Masala

Chat is an Indian salad snack sold on street stalls. This rather tart spice mixture is used to flavour the salad which can also be served as a refreshing first course before a main meal.

Makes 40 ml/2½ tbsp

INGREDIENTS

5 ml/1 tsp black peppercorns
5 ml/1 tsp cumin seeds
5 ml/1 tsp ajowan seeds
5 ml/1 tsp pomegranate seeds
5 ml/1 tsp mixed black salt and sea salt
1.5 ml/¼ tsp asafoetida
5 ml/1 tsp mango powder
2.5 ml/½ tsp cayenne pepper, or to taste
2.5 ml/½ tsp garam masala (optional)

1 Grind the peppercorns to a powder with the cumin, ajowan, pomegranate seeds and salts.

2 Add the remaining ingredients, adjusting the quantity of cayenne pepper to taste and omitting the garam masala, if preferred. Mix well.

cayenne pepper

sea salt

Malaysian Spice Paste

In Malaysia this fairly fiery paste is usually served with chicken.

Makes about 350 g/12 oz

INGREDIENTS

6 fresh red chillies, seeded and sliced
3 red Bombay onions or 12 shallots, roughly chopped
4 garlic cloves
2.5 cm/1 in piece fresh turmeric root, peeled and sliced or 1 tsp ground turmeric
10 candlenuts or macadamia nuts
2.5 cm/1 in cube of blachan, prepared
3 lemon grass stalks

1 Place the chillies, onions or shallots, garlic, turmeric, nuts and blachan in a food processor.

2 Trim the root end from the lemon grass and slice the lower 6 cm/2½ in bulbous section into small pieces.

3 Add the lemon grass to the remaining ingredients and process them to a fine paste. Use the paste at once or store in an airtight glass jar in the fridge for a few days or in a plastic container in the freezer.

macadamia nuts

fresh red chillies

lemon grass

Thai Red Curry Paste

This fairly fiery paste is usually served with meat and poultry, especially chicken dishes.

Makes about 175 g/6 oz

INGREDIENTS

2.5cm/1in piece fresh root ginger
4 shallots
4-6 garlic cloves
4 lemon grass stalks
4 fresh red chillies
20ml/4 tsp coriander seeds
10ml/2 tsp cumin seeds
10ml/2 tsp hot paprika
1.5ml/¼ tsp ground turmeric
2.5ml/½ tsp salt
grated rind and juice of 2 limes
15ml/1 tbsp vegetable oil

fresh red chillies

1 Peel and chop the ginger, shallots and garlic. Peel and finely chop the lemon grass. Wearing rubber gloves, remove the stalks from the chillies, then cut them in half lengthwise. Scrape out the seeds and fleshy white ribs, then coarsely chop the flesh.

2 Heat a small frying pan over a medium heat, then add the coriander and cumin seeds. Toss them in the pan until the spices turn a shade darker and emit a roasted aroma. Allow to cool.

3 Place all the ingredients in a blender or food processor and process to make a coarse paste. Store in a screw-top jar for up to 1 month in the fridge and use as required.

Thai Green Curry Paste

This is similar to the red paste, but has coriander leaves to strengthen the colour and flavour.

Makes about 175 g/6 oz

coriander

INGREDIENTS

6 spring onions
4 coriander stems, washed
4 kaffir lime leaves
6-8 green chillies
4 garlic cloves, chopped
2.5cm/1in piece fresh root ginger, chopped
1 lemon grass stalk, chopped
45ml/3 tbsp chopped fresh coriander
45ml/3 tbsp chopped fresh basil
15ml/1 tbsp vegetable oil

fresh green chillies

1 Chop the spring onions and coriander stems. Remove the centre vein from the kaffir lime leaves, then cut into fine shreds. Seed and chop the chillies.

2 Put all the ingredients in a food processor and process to make a smooth paste. Store in a screw-top jar for up to 2 weeks in the fridge and use as required.

Chilli Sambal

This sauce is fiercely hot, and it will irritate the skin, so should you get any on your fingers, immediately wash them well in soapy water.

Makes 450 g/1 lb

INGREDIENTS

450 g/1 lb red chillies, seeded
10 ml/2 tsp salt

1 Plunge the chillies into a large pan of boiling water and cook them for 5-8 minutes.

2 Drain the chillies and then grind them in a food processor or blender, without making the paste too smooth.

3 Turn the paste into a glass jar, stir in the salt and cover with a piece of greaseproof paper or clear film before screwing on the lid.

4 Store the sambal in the fridge. Spoon it into small dishes. Serve as an accompaniment.

red chillies

Harissa

This chilli-based condiment is widely used in Moroccan, Tunisian and Algerian cooking. It can be served as a side dish in which to dip pieces of grilled and barbecued meat, or it can be stirred into soups and tagines, adding a distinctive, spicy flavour.

Makes 120 ml/4 fl oz/½ cup

INGREDIENTS

12 dried red chillies
15 ml/1 tbsp coriander seeds
30 ml/2 tbsp cumin seeds
2 garlic cloves
2.5 ml/½ tsp salt
60-90 ml/4-6 tbsp olive oil

1 Discard the stems and some of the seeds from the chillies, then soak the chillies in warm water for 30 minutes, until softened.

2 Meanwhile, dry-fry the coriander and cumin seeds to bring out the flavour and grind them to a powder.

3 Pound the garlic with the salt, then add the drained chillies and pound the mixture until it is smooth.

4 Add the spices and gradually pound in the oil, trickling it in and mixing until the sauce is well blended and of a mayonnaise-like consistency.

5 Use the harissa at once or transfer it to an airtight jar. Flood the surface with a little more olive oil to make a seal. Cover closely and store in a cool place or in the fridge for up to 3 weeks.

coriander seeds

garlic

cumin seeds

Cajun Spice Mix

This spice mixture can be used as a seasoning for jambalaya and gumbo, as well as for fish steaks, chicken or meat.

Makes about 150 ml/¼ pint/⅔ cup

INGREDIENTS
5 ml/1 tsp black peppercorns
5 ml/1 tsp cumin seeds
5 ml/1 tsp white mustard seeds
10 ml/2 tsp paprika
5 ml/1 tsp chilli powder or
    cayenne pepper
5 ml/1 tsp dried oregano
10 ml/2 tsp dried thyme
5 ml/1 tsp salt
2 garlic cloves
1 onion, sliced

1 Dry-fry or roast the peppercorns, cumin and mustard seeds over a medium heat to release their flavours.

2 Grind the roasted spices to a fine powder, then add the paprika, chilli or cayenne pepper, oregano, thyme and salt and grind again.

3 If it is to be used immediately, add the spices to the garlic and onion and process in a blender or food processor until well combined.

dried thyme

black peppercorns

chilli powder

dried oregano

Chinese Five-spice Powder

Use this spice mixture in chicken, pork and red meat dishes with soy sauce and to season Chinese spareribs.

Makes about 75 ml/⅓ cup

INGREDIENTS
5 ml/1 tsp Szechuan pepper
5 ml/1 tsp cassia or ground
    cinnamon
5 ml/1 tsp cloves
5 ml/1 tsp fennel seeds
5 ml/1 tsp star anise

1 Grind all the ingredients to a fine powder and store in an airtight container.

star anise

cloves

Szechuan pepper

fennel seeds

cassia

SWEET SPICES

Pickling Spice

This traditional mixture can be bought ready-mixed, but keen cooks enjoy experimenting with different flavour combinations. Sometimes the spices are crushed before they are added to the mixture; for other recipes, the spices are tied.

Makes 120 ml/4 fl oz/½ cup

INGREDIENTS

15 ml/1 tbsp coriander seeds
15 ml/1 tbsp mustard seeds
15 ml/1 tbsp black or white
   peppercorns
15 ml/1 tbsp cloves
15 ml/1 tbsp allspice berries
3-4 dried red chillies
2.5 cm/1 in piece dried root ginger
2.5 cm/1 in piece cinnamon stick
   (optional)
3 dried bay leaves (optional)

1 Mix together all the spices. Place them in a piece of muslin and tie the ends securely.

2 Alternatively, place the spices in a stainless steel or enamelled saucepan and pour in vinegar. Heat gently until boiling, allow to cool, then strain the vinegar and discard the spices.

3 To make cold spice vinegar, add the spices to a jar or bottle of vinegar and leave to infuse for 1-2 days. Strain and use as required, discarding the spices.

cinnamon stick

coriander seeds

mustard seeds

white peppercorns

allspice berries

dried red chillies

dried root ginger

cloves

dried bay leaves

Apple Pie Spice

This spice mixture is a perfect flavouring combination for the universally popular apple pie. Some cooks prefer to use the cloves in their whole form. Use in stewed fruit, fruit sauces and fruit pies filled with plums, pears or rhubarb as well as apples.

Makes 25 ml/1½ tbsp

INGREDIENTS

5 ml/1 tsp ground or whole cloves
15 ml/1 tbsp ground cinnamon
2.5-5 ml/½-1 tsp freshly grated
   nutmeg

1 Mix the spices and use at once or store in an airtight container away from strong light.

ground cloves

grated nutmeg

ground cinnamon

Mixed Spice or Pudding Spice

This is another traditional spice mix, which can also be bought ready-ground. It is used in a variety of cakes and puddings, such as fruit cake, gingerbread and Christmas pudding. Make it up in small quantities as the mixture soon loses its rich flavour.

Makes 30 ml/2 tbsp

INGREDIENTS

5 ml/1 tsp allspice berries
2.5 cm/1 in cinnamon stick
5 ml/1 tsp cloves
5 ml/1 tsp freshly grated nutmeg
5 ml/1 tsp ground ginger

1 Grind the allspice, cinnamon and cloves to a fine powder and mix well with the nutmeg and ginger. Use at once or store in an airtight jar away from strong light.

allspice berries

cinnamon stick

cloves

grated nutmeg

ground ginger

Quatre Epices

As the name indicates, this is a blend of four spices; it is a favourite seasoning for French charcuterie and Arabian cooking. The proportions can be varied to suit the food or dish. Equivalent quantities of allspice and cinnamon can be substituted for the white pepper and ginger respectively.

Makes 80 ml/5-6 tsp

INGREDIENTS

45 ml/3 tbsp ground white pepper
15 ml/1 tbsp freshly grated nutmeg
5 ml/1 tsp ground cloves
15 ml/1 tbsp ground ginger

1 Mix all the spices together and use at once or store in an airtight jar away from strong light.

white pepper

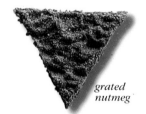

grated nutmeg

ground cloves

ground ginger

Hot and Sour Prawn Soup

How hot this soup is depends upon the type of chilli used. Try tiny Thai chilli if you really want to "go for the burn".

Serves 6

INGREDIENTS

225 g/8 oz raw prawns, in shells
2 lemon grass stalks
1.5 litres/2½ pints/6¼ cups
    vegetable stock
4 kaffir lime leaves
2 slices peeled fresh root ginger
60 ml/4 tbsp Thai fish sauce
60 ml/4 tbsp fresh lime juice
2 garlic cloves, crushed
6 spring onions, chopped
1 fresh red chilli, seeded and cut
    into thin strips
115 g/4 oz oyster mushrooms, sliced
fresh coriander leaves and kaffir
    lime slices, to garnish.

1 Peel the prawns and set them aside. Put the shells in a large saucepan.

oyster mushrooms

garlic

prawns

coriander

red chillies   *Thai fish sauce*

kaffir lime leaves   *lime juice*

vegetable stock   *kaffir lime slices*   *lemon grass*

ginger

spring onions

COOK'S TIP
It is important that the prawns are not overcooked, or they will become tough.

2 Lightly crush the lemon grass and add to the pan with the stock, lime leaves and ginger. Bring to the boil, lower the heat and simmer for 20 minutes.

3 Strain the stock into a clean pan discarding the prawn shells and aromatics. Add the fish sauce, lime juice, garlic, spring onions, chilli and mushrooms. Bring to the boil, lower the heat and simmer for 5 minutes. Add the peeled prawns and cook for 2-3 minutes. Serve, garnished with coriander leaves and kaffir lime slices.

Nachos with Chilli Beef

Nachos are a favourite Mexican snack. Served here with spicy beef and topped with cheese, they make a satisfying, quick meal.

Serves 4

INGREDIENTS

225 g/8 oz minced beef
2 red chillies, seeded and chopped
3 spring onions, chopped
175 g/6 oz nachos
300 ml/½ pint/1¼ cups soured cream
50 g/2oz Cheddar cheese, grated
salt and freshly ground black pepper

chillies   *cheese*

nachos

minced beef   *soured cream*

spring onions

1 Dry-fry the minced beef and chillies in a large pan for 10 minutes, stirring all the time.

2 Add the spring onions, season and cook for a further 5 minutes.

3 Arrange the nachos in four individual flameproof dishes. Preheat the grill.

4 Spoon on the beef mixture and top with soured cream and grated cheese. Grill under a medium grill for 5 minutes.

Hot Chilli Chicken

Not for the faint-hearted, this fiery, hot curry is made with a spicy chilli masala paste.

Serves 4

INGREDIENTS

30 ml/2 tbsp tomato purée
2 garlic cloves, roughly chopped
2 green chillies, roughly chopped
5 dried red chillies
2.5 ml/½ tsp salt
1.5 ml/¼ tsp sugar
5 ml/1 tsp chilli powder
2.5 ml/½ tsp paprika
15 ml/1 tbsp curry paste
30 ml/2 tbsp vegetable oil
2.5 ml/½ tsp cumin seeds
1 onion, finely chopped
2 bay leaves
5 ml/1 tsp ground coriander
5 ml/1 tsp ground cumin
1.5 ml/¼ tsp ground turmeric
400 g/14 oz can chopped tomatoes
8 chicken thighs, skinned
5 ml/1 tsp garam masala
sliced green chillies, to garnish
chappatis and natural yogurt,
    to serve

curry paste · ground coriander · onion · garlic · chicken thighs · green chillies · bay leaves · red chillies · garam masala · cumin seeds · chopped tomatoes · paprika

1 Put the tomato purée, garlic, green and dried red chillies, salt, sugar, chilli powder, paprika and curry paste into a food processor or blender and process to a smooth paste.

2 Heat the oil in a large saucepan and fry the cumin seeds for 2 minutes. Add the onion and bay leaves and fry for about 5 minutes.

3 Add the chilli paste and fry for 2-3 minutes. Add the remaining ground spices and cook for 2 minutes. Add the chopped tomatoes and 150 ml/1¼ pints/ ⅔ cup water. Bring to the boil and simmer for about 5 minutes until the sauce thickens.

4 Add the chicken and garam masala. Cover and simmer for 25-30 minutes until the chicken is tender. Garnish with sliced green chillies and serve with chappatis and natural yogurt.

Beef Madras

Madras curries originally came from southern India and are aromatic, robust and pungent in flavour. This recipe uses beef, but you could replace this with lamb if you prefer.

Serves 4

INGREDIENTS

900 g/2 lb stewing beef
45 ml/3 tbsp vegetable oil
1 large onion, finely chopped
4 cloves
4 green cardamom pods
2 fresh green chillies, seeded and
    finely chopped
2.5 cm/1 in piece fresh root ginger,
    finely chopped
2 garlic cloves, crushed
2 dried red chillies
15 ml/1 tbsp curry paste
10 ml/2 tsp ground coriander
5 ml/1 tsp ground cumin
2.5 ml/½ tsp salt
150 ml/¼ pint/⅔ cup beef stock
tomato rice, to serve
fresh coriander sprigs, to garnish

curry paste

red chillies

ground cumin

stewing beef

cloves

green chillies

vegetable oil

beef stock

salt

ground coriander

1 Remove any visible fat or gristle and cut the meat into 2.5 cm/1 in cubes.

2 Heat the oil in a large frying pan and fry the onion, cloves and cardamom pods for 5 minutes. Add the fresh green chillies, ginger, garlic and dried red chillies and fry for a further 2 minutes.

3 Add the curry paste and fry for about 2 minutes. Add the beef and fry for 5-8 minutes, stirring occasionally to turn the meat until all the pieces are lightly browned.

4 Add the coriander, cumin, salt and stock. Cover and simmer gently for 1-1½ hours or until the meat is tender. Serve with tomato rice and garnish with coriander sprigs.

Beef Vindaloo

A fiery hot dish originally from Goa, a "vindaloo" curry is made using a unique blend of hot aromatic spices and vinegar to give it a distinctive spicy flavour.

Serves 4

INGREDIENTS

15 ml/1 tbsp cumin seeds
4 dried red chillies
5 ml/1 tsp black peppercorns
5 green cardamom pods, seeds only
5 ml/1 tsp fenugreek seeds
5 ml/1 tsp black mustard seeds
2.5 ml/½ tsp salt
2.5 ml/½ tsp demerara sugar
60 ml/4 tbsp white wine vinegar
60 ml/4 tbsp vegetable oil
1 large onion, finely chopped
900 g/2 lb stewing beef, cut into 2.5
    cm/1 in cubes
2.5 cm/1 in piece fresh root ginger,
    finely chopped
1 garlic clove, crushed
10 ml/2 tsp ground coriander
2.5 ml/½ tsp ground turmeric
plain and yellow rice, to serve

1 Put the cumin seeds, chillies, peppercorns, cardamom seeds, fenugreek seeds and mustard seeds into a coffee grinder or use a pestle and mortar and grind to a fine powder. Transfer to a bowl. Add the salt, sugar and white wine vinegar and mix to a thin paste.

2 Heat 30 ml/2 tbsp of the oil in a large frying pan and fry the onion for 10 minutes. Put the onion and the spice mixture into a food processor or blender and process to a coarse paste.

oil
garlic
onion
white wine vinegar
root ginger
salt
red chillies
cardamom pods
ground turmeric
black peppercorns
demerara sugar
fenugreek seeds
black mustard seeds
stewing beef
cumin seeds
ground coriander

3 Heat the remaining oil in the frying pan and fry the meat cubes for about 10 minutes until lightly browned. Remove the beef cubes with a slotted spoon and set aside.

4 Add the ginger and garlic and fry for 2 minutes. Stir in the ground coriander and turmeric and fry for 2 minutes.

COOK'S TIP

To make plain and yellow rice, infuse a pinch of saffron strands or dissolve a little ground turmeric in 15 ml/1 tbsp hot water. Stir into half the cooked rice until uniformly yellow. Carefully mix the yellow rice into the plain rice.

5 Add the spice and onion paste and fry for about 5 minutes.

6 Return the meat to the pan together with 300 ml/½ pint/1¼ cups water. Cover and simmer for 1-1½ hours or until the meat is tender. Serve with plain and yellow rice.

Chilli Beef Tortilla

Perhaps the best-known Mexican recipe (called Chimichanga), these wheat tortillas are filled with chilli beef, topped with a spicy cheese sauce and served with traditional accompaniments.

Serves 4

INGREDIENTS

4 wheat tortillas

FOR THE FILLING
15 ml/1 tbsp olive oil
450 g/1 lb minced beef
1 onion, chopped
5 ml/1 tsp paprika
1 red chilli, seeded and sliced
15ml/1 tbsp plain flour
150 ml/¼ pint/⅔ cup beef stock
2 large tomatoes
salt and freshly ground black pepper
green peppers, chopped tomatoes,
    guacamole and soured cream,
    to serve

FOR THE CHEESE SAUCE
25 g/1 oz/2 tbsp butter
25 g/1 oz/2 tbsp plain flour
300 ml/½ pint/ 1¼ cups milk
50 g/2 oz/½ cup grated mature
    Cheddar cheese
pinch of paprika

red chilli

cheese

tortillas

minced beef

tomatoes

onion

1 Preheat the oven to 180°C/350°F/ Gas 4. For the filling, heat the oil in a large pan and fry the minced beef for 5 minutes. Add the onion and fry for a further 5 minutes.

2 Add the paprika, chilli and flour. Cook for 1 minute. Stir in the beef stock. Season well and bring to the boil. Then reduce the heat and simmer for 20 minutes.

3 For the cheese sauce, melt the butter in a pan and add the flour. Cook for 1 minute and gradually stir in the milk. Add the grated cheese and paprika, season to taste and bring to the boil, stirring continuously.

4 Chop the tomatoes. Place a little of the minced beef mixture along the length of each tortilla. Place the tomatoes on top, roll up into a "cigar" shape and place seam side down in an ovenproof dish. Pour the cheese sauce over each tortilla and cook in the preheated oven for 20 minutes. Serve with green peppers, chopped tomatoes, guacamole and soured cream, if liked.

Chilli and Lime Fish Cakes

Bursting with the zesty flavours of chillies and lime, these little fish cakes make a wonderfully piquant appetizer.

Serves 4

INGREDIENTS

450 g/1 lb white fish fillets, such as cod or haddock
3 spring onions, sliced
30 ml/2 tbsp chopped fresh coriander
30 ml/2 tbsp Thai red curry paste
1 green chilli, seeded and chopped
10 ml/2 tsp grated lime rind
15 ml/1 tbsp lime juice
30 ml/2 tbsp peanut oil
salt
crisp lettuce leaves, spring onions, sliced lengthways, thinly sliced chilli slices, coriander sprigs and lime wedges, to serve

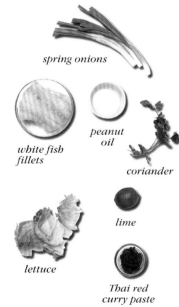

spring onions

white fish fillets

peanut oil

coriander

lettuce

lime

Thai red curry paste

1 Cut the fish into chunks, then place in a blender or food processor.

2 Add the spring onions, coriander, red curry paste, green chilli, lime rind and juice to the fish. Season with salt. Process until finely chopped.

3 Using lightly floured hands, divide the mixture into 16 pieces and shape each one into a small cake about 4 cm/1½ in across. Place the fish cakes on a plate, cover with clear film and chill for about 2 hours, until firm. Heat a wok over a high heat until hot. Add the oil and swirl it around.

4 Fry the fish cakes, a few at a time, for 6-8 minutes, turning them carefully until evenly browned. Drain each batch on kitchen paper and keep hot while cooking the remainder. Serve the fish cakes on a bed of crisp lettuce leaves with spring onions, red chilli slices, coriander sprigs and lime wedges.

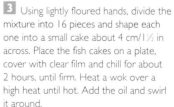

Spiced Coconut Mushrooms

Here is a simple and delicious way to give mushrooms an exotic spicy flavour. They may be served with grilled or roasted meats or poultry.

Serves 3-4

INGREDIENTS

30 ml/2 tbsp peanut oil
2 garlic cloves, finely chopped
2 red chillies, seeded and sliced into
     rings
3 shallots, finely chopped
225 g/8 oz button mushrooms,
     thickly sliced
150ml/¼ pint/⅔ cup coconut milk
30 ml/2 tbsp finely chopped fresh
     coriander
salt and freshly ground black pepper

button mushrooms *coriander*

shallots *garlic*
coconut milk

peanut oil
red chillies

1 Heat a wok until hot, add the oil and swirl it around. Add the garlic and chillies and stir-fry for a few seconds.

2 Add the finely chopped shallots and stir-fry for 2-3 minutes, until softened. Add the mushrooms and stir-fry for 3 minutes.

3 Pour in the coconut milk and bring to the boil. Boil rapidly over high heat until the liquid is reduced by half and coats the mushrooms. Taste and adjust the seasoning, if necessary.

4 Sprinkle over the coriander and toss gently to mix. Serve at once.

Baby Onions and Mushrooms à la Grecque

There are many variations of this classic dish, but all contain coriander seeds.

Serves 4

INGREDIENTS

2 carrots
350 g/12 oz baby onions
60 ml/4 tbsp olive oil
120 ml/4 fl oz/½ cup dry white wine
5ml/1 tsp coriander seeds, lightly
    crushed
2 bay leaves
pinch of cayenne pepper
1 garlic clove, crushed
375 g/12 oz button mushrooms
3 tomatoes, peeled, seeded and
    quartered
salt and freshly ground black pepper
45 ml/3 tbsp chopped fresh parsley,
    to garnish

garlic

button
mushrooms

white wine

bay leaves

tomatoes

baby onions

coriander
seeds

parsley

carrots

COOK'S TIP
Don't trim too much from either the top or root end of the onions: if you do, the centres will pop out during cooking.

1 Peel the carrots and cut them into small dice. Peel the baby onions and trim the tops and roots.

2 Heat 45ml/3 tbsp of the olive oil in a deep frying pan. Add the carrots and onions and cook, stirring occasionally, for about 20 minutes until the vegetables have browned lightly and are beginning to soften.

3 Add the white wine, coriander seeds, bay leaves, cayenne pepper, garlic, button mushrooms and tomatoes, and season to taste. Cook, uncovered, for 20-30 minutes until the vegetables are soft and the sauce has thickened.

4 Transfer to a serving dish and leave to cool. Cover and chill until needed. Just before serving, drizzle over the remaining olive oil and sprinkle with the chopped parsley. Serve with hunks of crusty bread.

Cumin and Coriander Spiced Fish Bites

These crispy, spicy fritters are based on a dish from Baltistan, India.

Serves 4

INGREDIENTS

10 ml/2 tsp cumin seeds
10 ml/2 tsp coriander seeds
1-2 dried red chillies
30 ml/2 tbsp vegetable oil
175g/6oz gram flour
5 ml/1 tsp salt
10 ml/2 tsp garam masala
peanut oil, for deep-frying
675 g/1½ lb fish fillets, such as cod,
   skinned, boned and cut into
   thick strips
mint sprigs and lime halves,
   to garnish

red chillies

cumin seeds

gram flour

garam masala

peanut oil

fish fillets

mint

vegetable oil

1 Crush the cumin, coriander and chillies, using a mortar and pestle. Heat the vegetable oil in a wok and stir-fry the spices for 1-2 minutes.

2 Put the gram flour, salt, spice mixture and garam masala in a bowl. Gradually stir in enough water, about 250 ml/8 fl oz/1 cup, to make a thick batter. Cover and allow to rest for 30 minutes.

3 Half-fill a wok with peanut oil and heat to 190°C/375°F. When the oil has reached the required temperature, dip the fish, a few pieces at a time, into the batter, gently shaking off any excess.

4 Deep-fry the fish in batches for 4-5 minutes, until golden brown. Drain on kitchen paper. Serve immediately, garnished with mint sprigs, and lime halves for squeezing over the fritters.

Thai Pork Satay with Spicy Sauce

Coriander and cumin are used in both the satay and the sauce, giving an authentic pungent flavour.

Serves 8

INGREDIENTS

½ small onion, finely chopped
2 garlic cloves, crushed
30 ml/2 tbsp lemon juice
15 ml/1 tbsp soy sauce
5 ml/1 tsp ground coriander
2.5 ml/½ tsp ground cumin
5 ml/1 tsp ground turmeric
30 ml/2 tbsp vegetable oil
450 g/1lb pork tenderloin
fresh coriander sprigs, to garnish
boiled rice, to serve

FOR THE SAUCE
50 g/2oz creamed coconut, chopped
60 ml/4 tbsp crunchy peanut butter
15 ml/1 tbsp lemon juice
2.5 ml/½ tsp ground cumin
2.5 ml/½ tsp ground coriander
5 ml/1 tsp soft brown sugar
15 ml/1 tbsp soy sauce
1-2 dried red chillies, or ½ red chilli,
   seeded and finely chopped
15 ml/1 tbsp chopped fresh
   coriander

FOR THE SALAD
½ small cucumber, peeled, diced
15 ml/1 tbsp white wine vinegar
15 ml/1 tbsp chopped fresh
   coriander
salt and freshly ground black pepper

1 Soak eight wooden skewers in water for about 30 minutes – this will prevent them from charring during grilling.

2 Place the onion, garlic, lemon juice, soy sauce, ground spices and oil in a food processor or blender and pulse until smooth. Alternatively, mix in a large bowl.

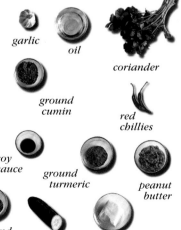

garlic

oil

coriander

ground cumin

red chillies

soy sauce

ground turmeric

peanut butter

pork tenderloin

rice

soft brown sugar

ground coriander

cucumber

creamed coconut

3 Using a sharp knife, cut the pork into thin strips and place in a deep bowl, then spoon over the marinade and mix well. Cover and chill for at least 2 hours.

4 Preheat the grill to the hottest setting. Thread about two or three pieces of pork on to each skewer and grill on a rack for 2-3 minutes each side, basting once with the marinade.

5 To make the sauce, dissolve the creamed coconut in 150 ml/¼ pint/⅔ cup of boiling water. Put the remaining ingredients into a pan and stir in the coconut liquid. Bring to the boil, then simmer for 5 minutes, until thick. Mix the salad. Place the satay sticks on a plate and serve with the sauce, salad and rice.

Jeera Chicken

An aromatic dish with a delicious, distinctive taste of cumin. Serve simply with a salad and yogurt.

Serves 4

INGREDIENTS

45 ml/3 tbsp cumin seeds
45 ml/3 tbsp vegetable oil
2.5 ml/½ tsp black peppercorns
4 green cardamom pods
2 green chillies, seeded and finely
    chopped
2 garlic cloves, crushed
2.5 cm/1 in piece fresh root ginger,
    grated
5 ml/1 tsp ground coriander
10 ml/2 tsp ground cumin
2.5 ml/½ tsp salt
8 chicken pieces, such as thighs and
    drumsticks, skinned
5 ml/1 tsp garam masala
fresh coriander and chilli powder,
    to garnish
cucumber raita, to serve

vegetable oil

black peppercorns

ground coriander

ground cumin

garam masala

cumin seeds

green chillies

chicken pieces

fresh root ginger

garlic

green cardamom pods

salt

1 Dry-roast 15 ml/1 tbsp of the cumin seeds for 5 minutes and set aside.

2 Heat the oil in a large saucepan and fry the remaining cumin seeds, black peppercorns and cardamoms for about 2-3 minutes.

3 Add the chillies, garlic and ginger and fry for 2 minutes. Add the ground coriander, cumin and salt and cook for 2-3 minutes.

4 Add the chicken pieces, then cover and simmer for 20-25 minutes.

5 Add the garam masala and reserved cumin seeds and cook for a further 5 minutes. Garnish with chilli powder and coriander and serve with cucumber raita.

Cardamom and Cumin Spiced Mushrooms

This mushroom dish makes an ideal accompaniment.

Serves 4

INGREDIENTS

30 ml/2 tbsp vegetable oil
2.5 ml/½ tsp cumin seeds
1.5 ml/¼ tsp black peppercorns
4 green cardamom pods
1.5 ml/¼ tsp ground turmeric
1 onion, finely chopped
5 ml/1 tsp ground cumin
5 ml/1 tsp ground coriander
2.5 ml/½ tsp garam masala
1 green chilli, seeded and finely
    chopped
2 garlic cloves, crushed
2.5 cm/1 in piece fresh root ginger,
    grated
400 g/14 oz can chopped tomatoes
1.5 ml/¼ tsp salt
450 g/1 lb button mushrooms,
    halved
chopped fresh coriander, to garnish

ground turmeric

cumin seeds

vegetable oil

black peppercorns

garam masala

ground cumin

ground coriander

onion

salt

root ginger

garlic

chopped tomatoes

cardamom pods

button mushrooms

green chilli

1 Heat the oil in a large saucepan or wok and fry the cumin seeds, peppercorns, cardamom pods and turmeric for 2-3 minutes.

2 Add the onion and fry for about 5 minutes until golden. Stir in the cumin, coriander and garam masala and fry for a further 2 minutes.

3 Add the chilli, garlic and ginger and fry for 2-3 minutes stirring all the time to prevent the spices from sticking to the pan. Add the tomatoes and salt. Bring to the boil and simmer for 5 minutes.

4 Add the halved mushrooms. Cover and simmer over a low heat for 10 minutes. Garnish with plenty of chopped fresh coriander.

Coriander Brioches

The warm flavour of coriander combines particularly well with orange in this recipe.

Makes 12

INGREDIENTS

225 g/8 oz strong white bread flour
10 ml/2 tsp easy-blend dried yeast
2.5 ml/½ tsp salt
15 ml/1 tbsp caster sugar
10 ml/2 tsp coriander seeds,
   coarsely ground
grated rind of 1 orange, plus extra
   to decorate
30ml/2 tbsp hand-hot water
2 eggs, beaten
50 g/2 oz unsalted butter, melted
1 small egg, beaten, to glaze

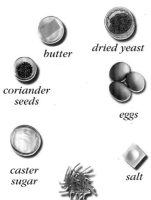

butter   *dried yeast*

*coriander
seeds*

eggs

*caster
sugar*   *salt*

rind of 1 orange

COOK'S TIP

These individual brioches look particularly attractive if they are made in special brioche tins. However, they can also be made in bun tins or muffin tins.

1 Sift the flour into a bowl and stir in the yeast, salt, sugar, coriander seeds and orange rind. Add the water, eggs and butter. Beat to make a soft dough. Turn on to a lightly floured surface and knead for 5 minutes, then place in a lightly oiled bowl, cover and leave in a warm place for 1 hour until doubled in bulk.

2 Turn on to a floured surface, knead again briefly and roll into a sausage. Cut into 12 pieces. Break off a quarter of each piece and set aside. Shape the larger pieces of dough into balls and place in 12 greased individual brioche tins.

3 Lightly flour your hands and roll each of the small pieces of dough into small sausages. Then lightly flour the handle of a wooden spoon and press in to the centre of each of the large dough balls to make a small hole. Place the dough sausages into the holes made by the spoon handle.

4 Place the brioche tins on a baking sheet. Cover with lightly oiled clear film and leave in a warm place until the dough rises almost to the top of the tins. Preheat the oven to 220°C/425°F/Gas 7. Brush the brioches with beaten egg and bake for 15 minutes until golden brown. Scatter over extra orange rind to decorate, and serve the brioches warm.

Pear Tart Tatin with Cardamom

Cardamom is a versatile spice which is good with sweet or savoury dishes. It is delicious with pears.

Serves 2-4

INGREDIENTS

50 g/2 oz butter, melted
50 g/2 oz caster sugar
seeds from 10 cardamom pods
225 g/8 oz puff pastry, thawed if
    frozen
4-5 ripe pears
cream, to serve

caster sugar *butter*

cardamom pods *puff pastry*

pears

1 Preheat the oven to 220°C/425°F/Gas 7. Spread the butter over the base of an 18 cm/7 in flameproof round tin, sprinkle with the sugar and scatter over the cardamom seeds. Roll out the pastry to a circle slightly larger than the tin, prick the pastry lightly and chill.

COOK'S TIP
You will need to use a heavy-based tin for this recipe. If you do not have a heavy cake tin, use an ovenproof omelette pan.

2 Peel, core and halve the pears lengthways. Arrange the pears, rounded side down, on the butter and sugar. Set the pan over a medium heat until the sugar melts and begins to bubble. If any areas are browning more than others, move the pan, but do not stir.

3 As soon as the sugar has caramelized, quickly remove the pan from the heat, so that the sugar does not burn. Place the pastry on top, tucking the edges down the side of the pan. Bake in the oven for 25 minutes until the pastry is well risen and golden.

4 Leave the tart in the pan for 2-3 minutes until the juices have stopped bubbling. Invert over a plate and shake to release the tart. It may be necessary to slide a spatula underneath the pears to loosen them. Serve the tart warm with cream.

Madras Sambal

There are many variations of this dish, but it is regularly cooked in almost every southern Indian home and served as part of a meal. You can use any combination of vegetables that are in season.

Serves 4

INGREDIENTS

225 g/8 oz toovar dhal or red split
    lentils
2.5 ml/½ tsp ground turmeric
2 large potatoes, cut into 2.5 cm/1
    in chunks
30 ml/2 tbsp vegetable oil
2.5 ml/½ tsp black mustard seeds
1.5 ml/¼ tsp fenugreek seeds
4 curry leaves
1 onion, thinly sliced
115 g/4 oz French beans, cut into
    2.5 cm/1 in lengths
5 ml/1 tsp salt
2.5 ml/½ tsp chilli powder
15 ml/1 tbsp lemon juice
60 ml/4 tbsp desiccated coconut
toasted coconut, to garnish
coriander chutney, to serve

1 Wash the toovar dhal or lentils in several changes of cold water. Place in a heavy-based saucepan with 600ml/ 1 pint/2½ cups water and turmeric. Cover and simmer for 30-35 minutes until the lentils are soft.

toovar dhal

black mustard seeds

fenugreek seeds

chilli powder

desiccated coconut

potatoes

ground turmeric

lemon juice

onion

salt

curry leaves

French beans

2 Par-boil the potatoes in a large pan of boiling water for 10 minutes. Drain well and set aside.

3 Heat the oil in a large frying pan and fry the mustard seeds, fenugreek seeds and curry leaves for 2-3 minutes until the seeds begin to splutter. Add the onion and the French beans and fry for 7-8 minutes. Add the potatoes and cook for a further 2 minutes.

4 Stir in the lentils with the salt, chilli powder and lemon juice and simmer for 2 minutes. Stir in the desiccated coconut and simmer for 5 minutes. Sprinkle over the toasted coconut and serve with a bowl of coriander chutney on the side.

Curried Smoked Fish Kedgeree

An ideal breakfast dish on a cold morning. Garnish with quartered hard-boiled eggs and season well.

Serves 6

INGREDIENTS

450 g/1 lb mixed smoked fish such
    as smoked cod, smoked haddock,
    smoked mussels or oysters if
    available
300 ml/½ pint/1¼ cups milk
175 g/6 oz long grain rice
1 slice of lemon
50 g/2 oz butter
5 ml/1 tsp medium curry powder
2.5 ml/½ tsp freshly grated nutmeg
15 ml/1 tbsp chopped fresh parsley
freshly ground black pepper
2 eggs, hard-boiled, and toast to serve

parsley

rice

smoked fish

lemon

nutmeg

curry powder

butter

1 Poach the uncooked smoked fish in milk for 10 minutes or until it flakes. Drain off the milk and flake the fish. Mix with other smoked fish.

2 Cook the rice in boiling water together with a slice of lemon for 10 minutes until just cooked. Drain well.

3 Melt the butter in a large heavy-based saucepan, add the rice and fish. Shake the saucepan to mix all the ingredients together thoroughly.

4 Gently stir in the curry powder, nutmeg and parsley. Season with freshly ground black pepper. Serve garnished with quartered eggs and toast.

Fish Curry

Any mixture of white fish works well with this fresh curry. Serve with warm naan bread to mop up the delicious juices.

Serves 4

INGREDIENTS

675 g/1½ lb white boneless fish such
    as halibut, cod, coley or monkfish
juice of ½ lime
5 ml/2 tsp cider vinegar
225 g/8 oz fresh coconut, chopped
2.5 cm/1 in piece of fresh root
    ginger, peeled and grated
6 garlic cloves
450 g/1 lb tomatoes, chopped
45 ml/3 tbsp sunflower oil
350 g/12 oz onions, roughly
    chopped
20 curry leaves
5 ml/1 tsp ground coriander
2.5 ml/½ tsp ground turmeric
10 ml/2 tsp ground chilli
2.5 ml/½ tsp fenugreek seeds
2.5 ml/½ tsp cumin seeds
salt and freshly ground black pepper
banana leaves, to serve
lime slices, to garnish

lime　*fresh root ginger*

onion

*cider
vinegar*

white fish

tomato

fresh coconut　*garlic*　*curry
leaves*

1 Marinate the fish in the lime juice, vinegar and a pinch of salt for about 30 minutes.

2 In a food processor or blender, process the chopped coconut, ginger, garlic and tomatoes to make a paste.

3 Heat the oil in a frying pan, add the onions and cook until golden brown, then add the curry leaves.

4 Add the coriander, turmeric and chilli and stir-fry for 1 minute.

5 Add the coconut paste and cook for 3-4 minutes, constantly stirring. Pour in 300 ml/½ pint/1¼ cups water, bring to the boil, and simmer for 4 minutes.

6 Pound the fenugreek and cumin seeds together in a pestle and mortar. Lay the fish on top of the simmering sauce, sprinkle over the fenugreek mixture and cook for 15 minutes or until the fish is tender. Serve garnished with lime slices.

Chicken Biriani

This is a good dish for entertaining. It can be prepared in advance and reheated in the oven. Serve with traditional curry accompaniments.

Serves 8

INGREDIENTS

900 g/2 lb boneless chicken thighs
60 ml/4 tbsp olive oil
2 large onions, thinly sliced
1-2 green chillies, seeded and finely
  chopped
5 ml/1 tsp grated fresh root ginger
1 garlic clove, crushed
15 ml/1 tbsp hot curry powder
150 ml/¼ pint/⅔ cup chicken stock
150 ml/¼ pint/⅔ cup natural low-fat
  yogurt
30 ml/2 tbsp chopped fresh
  coriander
salt and freshly ground black pepper

FOR THE SPICED RICE
450 g/1 lb basmati rice
2.5 ml/½ tsp garam masala
900 ml/1½ pints/3¾ cups chicken
  stock or water
50 g/2 oz raisins or sultanas
25 g/1 oz toasted almonds

1 Put the basmati rice into a sieve and wash under cold running water to remove any starchy powder coating the grains. Then put into a bowl and cover with cold water and soak for 30 minutes. The grains will absorb some water so that they will not stick together in a solid mass while cooking.

curry powder

chicken
thighs

fresh root ginger

chillies

coriander

almonds

basmati rice

yogurt

2 Preheat the oven to 160°C/325°F/Gas 3. Cut the chicken into cubes of approximately 2.5 cm/1 in. Heat 30 ml/2 tbsp of the oil in a large flameproof casserole, add one onion and cook until softened. Add the finely chopped chillies, ginger, garlic and curry powder and cook for a further 2 minutes, stirring occasionally.

3 Add the stock and seasoning, and bring slowly to the boil. Add the chicken pieces, cover and continue cooking in the oven for 20 minutes or until tender.

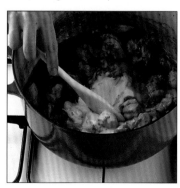

4 Remove the pan from the oven and then gently stir in the yogurt.

COOK'S TIP
Cover with buttered foil and bake in the oven for 30 minutes to reheat.

5 Meanwhile, heat the remaining oil in a flameproof casserole and cook the remaining sliced onion gently until lightly browned. Add the drained rice, garam masala and stock or water. Bring to the boil, cover and cook in the oven for 20-35 minutes or until the rice is tender and all the stock has been absorbed.

6 To serve, stir the raisins or sultanas and toasted almonds into the rice. Spoon half the rice into a large deep serving dish, cover with the chicken and then the remaining rice. Sprinkle with chopped coriander to garnish.

Chicken and Tomato Balti

If you like tomatoes, you will love this chicken recipe. It makes a semi-dry balti and is good served with a lentil dish and plain boiled rice.

Serves 4

INGREDIENTS

60ml/4 tbsp corn oil
6 curry leaves
2.5 ml/½ tsp mixed onion and mustard seeds
8 medium tomatoes, sliced
5 ml/1 tsp ground coriander
5 ml/1 tsp chilli powder
5 ml/1 tsp salt
5 ml/1 tsp ground cumin
5 ml/1 tsp garlic pulp
675 g/1½ lb chicken, skinned, boned and cubed
15 ml/1 tbsp sesame seeds, roasted
15 ml/1 tbsp chopped fresh coriander

corn oil
garlic
curry leaves
chilli powder
fresh coriander
sesame seeds
chicken, skinned
ground coriander
mixed onion and mustard seeds
ground cumin
tomatoes

1 Heat the corn oil in a deep round-bottomed frying pan or a medium karahi until the oil is just smoking. Add all of the curry leaves and mixed onion and mustard seeds and stir thoroughly to combine.

2 Stir-fry for about 30 seconds, then lower the heat and add the tomatoes.

3 While the tomatoes are cooking, mix together the coriander, chilli powder, salt, cumin and garlic. Tip the spice mixture over the tomatoes.

4 Add the chicken and stir. Stir-fry for about 5 minutes until the chicken is lightly browned. Pour on 150 ml/1¼ pints/⅔ cup water and continue cooking, stirring occasionally, until the sauce thickens and the chicken is cooked.

5 Generously sprinkle the sesame seeds and the chopped fresh coriander over the top of the dish and serve.

COOK'S TIP

Sesame seeds are available from Asian and health food stores. There are two types – unroasted seeds, which are white, and roasted ones, which are lightly browned. To roast sesame seeds at home, simply tip some into a dry frying pan and fry over a high heat for about 1 minute. Shake the pan constantly to prevent the seeds burning.

Mixed Vegetable Curry

A good all-round vegetable curry that goes well with most Indian meat dishes. You can use any combination of vegetables that are in season.

Serves 4

INGREDIENTS

30 ml/2 tbsp vegetable oil
2.5 ml/½ tsp black mustard seeds
2.5 ml/½ tsp cumin seeds
1 onion, thinly sliced
2 curry leaves
1 green chilli, seeded and finely chopped
2.5 cm/1 in piece fresh root ginger, finely chopped
30 ml/2 tbsp curry paste
1 small cauliflower, broken into florets
1 large carrot, thickly sliced
115 g/4 oz French beans, cut into 2.5 cm/1 in lengths
1.5 ml/¼ tsp ground turmeric
1.5 ml/¼ tsp chilli powder
2.5 ml/½ tsp salt
2 tomatoes, finely chopped
50 g/2 oz frozen peas, thawed
150 ml/¼ pint/⅔ cup vegetable stock
fresh curry leaves, to garnish

vegetable stock

curry paste

peas

chilli powder

mustard seeds

cauliflower

ground turmeric

cumin seeds

tomatoes

onion

curry leaves

carrot

fresh root ginger

green chilli

French beans

1 Heat the oil in a large saucepan and fry the mustard seeds and cumin seeds for 2 minutes until they begin to splutter.

2 Add the onion and curry leaves and fry for 5 minutes.

3 Add the chilli and ginger and fry for 2 minutes. Stir in the curry paste and fry for 3-4 minutes.

4 Add the cauliflower, carrot and French beans and cook for 4-5 minutes, then add the turmeric, chilli powder, salt and tomatoes and cook for 2-3 minutes.

5 Stir in the thawed peas and cook for a further 2-3 minutes.

6 Add the stock, cover and simmer over a low heat for 10-13 minutes until all the vegetables are tender. Serve, garnished with curry leaves.

Gingered Chicken Noodles

A blend of ginger, spices and coconut milk flavours this delicious supper dish, which is made in minutes. For a real oriental touch, add a little fish sauce to taste, just before serving.

Serves 4

INGREDIENTS

350 g/12 oz boneless, skinless
  chicken breasts
225 g/8 oz courgettes
275 g/10 oz aubergine
about 30 ml/2 tbsp vegetable oil
5 cm/2 in piece fresh root ginger,
  peeled and finely chopped
6 spring onions, sliced
10 ml/2 tsp Thai green curry paste
400 ml/14 fl oz/1⅔ cups coconut
  milk
475 ml/16 fl oz/2 cups chicken stock
115 g/4 oz medium egg noodles
45 ml/3 tbsp chopped fresh
  coriander
15 ml/1 tbsp lemon juice
salt and freshly ground black pepper
chopped fresh coriander, to garnish

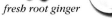

egg
noodles

lemon

chicken
breasts

coriander

aubergine

spring
onions

oil

Thai green
curry paste

chicken
stock

fresh root ginger

courgette

coconut
milk

1 Cut the chicken into bite-sized pieces. Halve the courgettes lengthways and roughly chop them. Cut the aubergine into similarly sized pieces.

2 Heat the oil in a large saucepan and fry the chicken until golden. Remove with a slotted spoon and drain.

3 Add a little more oil, if necessary, and stir-fry the ginger and spring onions for 3 minutes. Add the courgettes and cook for 2-3 minutes, or until beginning to turn golden. Stir in the curry paste and cook for 1 minute.

4 Add the coconut milk, stock, aubergine and chicken and simmer for 10 minutes. Add the noodles and cook for a further 5 minutes, or until the chicken is cooked and the noodles are tender. Stir in the coriander and lemon juice and adjust the seasoning. Serve garnished with chopped fresh coriander.

Seafood Stir-fry with Ginger

Served with plenty of crusty bread to mop up the juices and a glass of chilled dry white wine, this would make a refreshing summer supper.

Serves 2

INGREDIENTS

15 ml/1 tbsp sunflower oil
5 ml/1 tsp sesame oil
2.5 cm/1 in piece fresh root ginger, peeled and finely chopped
1 bunch spring onions, sliced
1 red pepper, seeded and finely chopped
115 g/4 oz small "queen" scallops
8 large uncooked prawns, shelled
115 g/4 oz squid rings
15 ml/1 tbsp lime juice
15 ml/1 tbsp light soy sauce
60 ml/4 tbsp coconut milk
salt and freshly ground pepper
mixed salad leaves and crusty bread, to serve

salad leaves

spring onions

fresh root ginger

red pepper

uncooked prawns

"queen" scallops

squid rings

light soy sauce
sunflower oil

sesame oil *lime* *coconut milk*

1 Heat the oils in a wok or large frying pan and cook the ginger and spring onions for 2-3 minutes, or until golden. Stir in the red pepper and cook for a further 3 minutes.

2 Add the scallops, prawns and squid rings and cook over a medium heat for about 3 minutes, until the seafood is just cooked, being careful not to overcook.

3 Stir in the lime juice, soy sauce and coconut milk and simmer, uncovered, for 2 minutes, until the juices begin to thicken slightly.

4 Season well. Arrange the salad leaves on serving plates and spoon over the seafood mixture with the juices. Serve with crusty bread.

Ginger and Lemon Grass Scented Mussels

The warming flavours of ginger and lemon grass are used in this quick and easy dish.

Serves 4

INGREDIENTS

1.75 kg/4-4½ lb fresh mussels in the shell
2 lemon grass stalks
handful of small fresh basil leaves
5 cm/2 in piece fresh root ginger
2 shallots, finely chopped
150 ml/¼ pint/⅔ cup fish stock

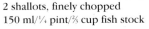

basil

mussels

fresh root ginger

shallots

lemon grass

fish stock

COOK'S TIP
Mussels are best bought fresh and eaten on the day of purchase. Any that remain closed after cooking should be thrown away.

1 Scrub the mussels under cold running water, scraping off any barnacles with a small sharp knife. Pull or cut off the hairy "beards". Discard any with damaged shells and any that remain closed when sharply tapped.

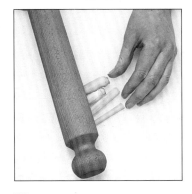

2 Cut each lemon grass stalk in half and bruise with a rolling pin.

3 Coarsely chop half the basil leaves; reserve the remainder for the garnish.

4 Put the mussels, lemon grass, basil, ginger, shallots and stock in a wok. Bring to a boil, cover and simmer for 5 minutes. Discard any mussels that remain closed. Sprinkle over the basil and serve.

Courgettes in Gingery Orange Sauce

If baby courgettes are unavailable, use larger ones, but cook whole so that they don't absorb too much water. Once cooked, halve them lengthways and cut into 10 cm/4 in lengths.

Serves 4

INGREDIENTS

350 g/12 oz baby courgettes
4 spring onions, finely sliced
2.5 cm/1 in fresh root ginger, grated
30 ml/2 tbsp cider vinegar
15 ml/1 tbsp light soy sauce
5 ml/1 tsp soft light brown sugar
45 ml/3 tbsp vegetable stock
finely grated rind and juice of
 ½ lemon and ½ orange
5 ml/1 tsp cornflour
salt

orange

courgettes

lemon

fresh root ginger

spring onions

1 Cook the courgettes in lightly salted boiling water for 3-4 minutes, or until just tender. Drain well and return to pan.

2 Meanwhile put all the remaining ingredients, except the cornflour, into a small saucepan and bring to the boil. Simmer for 3 minutes.

3 Blend the cornflour with 10ml/2 tsp of cold water and add to the sauce. Bring to the boil, stirring continuously, until the sauce has thickened.

4 Pour the sauce over the courgettes and heat gently, shaking the pan to coat evenly. Transfer to a warmed serving dish and serve.

Spicy Chick-peas with Fresh Ginger

Chick-peas are filling, nourishing and cheap. Here they are cooked with abundant spices and served with a refreshing raita made with spring onions and mint.

Serves 4-6

INGREDIENTS

225 g/8 oz dried chick-peas
30 ml/2 tbsp vegetable oil
1 small onion, chopped
4 cm/1½ in piece fresh root ginger, finely chopped
2 garlic cloves, finely chopped
1.5 ml/¼ tsp ground turmeric
450 g/1 lb tomatoes, peeled, seeded and chopped
30 ml/2 tbsp finely chopped fresh coriander
10 ml/2 tsp garam masala
salt and freshly ground black pepper
fresh coriander sprigs to garnish

FOR THE RAITA

150ml/¼ pint/⅔ cup natural yogurt
2 spring onions, finely chopped
5 ml/1 tsp roasted cumin seeds
30 ml/2 tbsp chopped fresh mint
pinch of cayenne pepper, or to taste

coriander

onion

fresh root ginger

turmeric *yogurt*

garam masala *cumin seeds*

garlic

spring onions *mint* *tomatoes*

1 Put the chick-peas in a large bowl and pour over enough cold water to cover. Soak overnight. The next day, drain the chick-peas and put them in a large pan with cold water to cover. Bring to the boil, and boil for 10 minutes, then lower the heat and simmer gently for 1-2 hours, until tender. Drain well.

2 Heat a karahi or wok until hot and add the oil. Add the onion and stir-fry for 2-3 minutes, then add the ginger, garlic and turmeric. Stir-fry for a few seconds more. Add the tomatoes, chick-peas and seasoning, bring to a boil, then simmer for 10-15 minutes until the tomatoes have reduced to a thick sauce.

3 Meanwhile, make the raita: mix together the yogurt, spring onions, roasted cumin seeds, mint and cayenne pepper to taste. Set aside.

4 Just before the end of cooking, stir in the chopped coriander and garam masala. Serve garnished with coriander sprigs and accompanied by the raita.

Gingercake

Three forms of ginger make this the ultimate cake for all lovers of this versatile spice.

Makes 12 squares

INGREDIENTS

225 g/8 oz self-raising flour
15 ml/1 tbsp ground ginger
5 ml/1 tsp ground cinnamon
2.5 ml/½ tsp bicarbonate of soda
115 g/4 oz butter
115 g/4 oz soft light brown sugar
2 eggs
25 ml/1½ tbsp golden syrup
25 ml/1½ tbsp milk

FOR THE TOPPING
6 pieces stem ginger, plus 20ml/
    4 tsp syrup, from the jar
115 g/4 oz icing sugar
lemon juice

brown sugar

ground ginger

*bicarbonate
of soda*

butter

icing sugar

*lemon
juice*

milk

*ground
cinnamon*

eggs

golden syrup

1 Preheat the oven to 160°C/325°F/ Gas 3. Grease a shallow 18 cm/7 in square cake tin and line with non-stick baking paper.

2 Sift the flour, ginger, cinnamon and bicarbonate of soda into a bowl. Rub in the butter, then stir in the sugar. Make a well in the centre. Whisk together the eggs, syrup and milk and pour into the bowl. Beat until smooth and glossy.

3 Spoon into the prepared tin and bake for 45-50 minutes until well risen. Leave in the tin for 30 minutes, then remove to a wire rack to cool completely.

4 Cut each piece of stem ginger into quarters and arrange the pieces on top of the cake.

5 Sift the icing sugar into a bowl and stir in the ginger syrup and enough lemon juice to make a smooth icing. Spoon the icing into a greaseproof paper icing bag and drizzle over the top of the cake. Leave to set, then cut the cake into squares.

COOK'S TIP
This cake will be even more delicious if it is kept in an airtight tin for a day before eating.

Ginger and Lemon Puddings with Custard

The flavours of lemon and ginger complement each other perfectly in these light little puddings.

Serves 8

INGREDIENTS

3 lemons
75 g/3 oz drained stem ginger, plus
    30ml/2 tbsp syrup from the jar
60ml/4 tbsp golden syrup
175 g/6 oz self-raising flour
10 ml/2 tsp ground ginger
115 g/4 oz butter, softened
115 g/4 oz caster sugar
2 eggs, beaten
45-60ml/3-4 tbsp milk

FOR THE VANILLA CUSTARD

150 ml/¼ pint/⅔ cup milk
150 ml/¼ pint/⅔ cup double cream
1 vanilla pod, split
3 egg yolks
5ml/1 tsp cornflour
25 g/1 oz caster sugar

1 Preheat the oven to 160°C/325°F/ Gas 3. Grease 8 individual pudding basins. Set one lemon aside for the sauce. Grate the rind from the remaining lemons and reserve. Remove all the pith from one of the grated lemons and slice into 8 thin rounds. Squeeze the juice from the second grated lemon. Chop the stem ginger.

2 Mix 15ml/1 tbsp of the ginger syrup with 30ml/2 tbsp of the golden syrup and 5ml/1 tsp of the lemon juice. Divide among the greased pudding basins. Place a slice of lemon in the bottom of each basin.

3 Sift the flour and ground ginger into a bowl. In a separate bowl, beat the butter and sugar together until pale and fluffy. Beat in the eggs, then fold in the flour mixture. Add enough milk to give a soft consistency, then stir in the lemon rind. Spoon into the pudding basins.

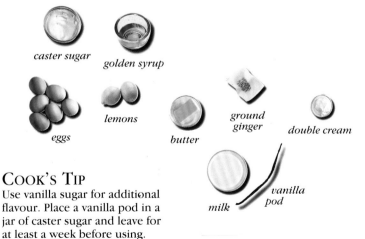

caster sugar   golden syrup

eggs   lemons   butter   ground ginger   double cream

milk   vanilla pod

COOK'S TIP
Use vanilla sugar for additional flavour. Place a vanilla pod in a jar of caster sugar and leave for at least a week before using.

4 Cover each basin with foil and stand in a roasting tin. Add boiling water to come halfway up the basins. Overwrap with foil, sealing well. Bake for 30-45 minutes, until cooked through.

5 To make the lemon and ginger sauce, grate the rind and squeeze the juice from the remaining lemon. Place in a pan with the remaining ginger syrup and golden syrup, bring to the boil, and simmer for 2 minutes. Keep warm.

6 To make the custard, mix the milk and cream in a pan. Add the vanilla pod and heat until almost boiling. Remove from the heat and leave for 10 minutes. Whisk together the egg yolks, cornflour and sugar, then strain into the milk and cream. Whisk until blended, then return to the clean pan and heat, stirring, until thick. Turn out the puddings, spoon over the sauce and serve with the custard.

GARLIC

Mellow Garlic Dip

Two whole heads of garlic may seem like a lot, but, once cooked, they become sweet and mellow. Serve with crunchy bread sticks and crisps.

Serves 4

COOK'S TIP
If you are having a barbecue, roast the garlic heads whole on the grill until tender. The cloves can then be separated before peeling and mashing.

INGREDIENTS

2 whole garlic heads
15 ml/1 tbsp olive oil
60 ml/4 tbsp mayonnaise
75 ml/5 tbsp Greek-style yogurt
5 ml/1 tsp wholegrain mustard
salt and freshly ground black pepper

garlic heads   *olive oil*

mayonnaise   *Greek-style yogurt*

wholegrain mustard

1 Preheat the oven to 200°C/400°F/Gas 6. Separate the garlic cloves and place them in a small roasting tin.

2 Pour the olive oil over the garlic cloves and turn them with a spoon to coat them evenly. Roast for 20-30 minutes, until the garlic is tender and softened. Leave to cool for 5 minutes.

3 Trim off the root end of each roasted garlic clove. Peel the cloves and discard the skins.

4 Place the roasted garlic on a chopping board and sprinkle with salt. Mash with a fork until puréed.

5 Place the garlic in a small bowl and stir in the mayonnaise, yogurt and wholegrain mustard.

6 Check and adjust the seasoning, and spoon the dip into a bowl. Cover and chill until ready to serve.

VARIATION
For a low-fat version of this dip, use reduced-fat mayonnaise and low-fat natural yogurt.

Roasted Garlic Toasts

A delicious starter or accompaniment to meat or vegetable dishes.

Serves 4

INGREDIENTS

2 whole garlic heads
fresh rosemary sprigs
extra-virgin olive oil
ciabatta loaf or thick baguette
chopped fresh rosemary
salt and freshly ground black pepper

1 Preheat the oven to 200°C/400°F/ Gas 6. Slice the tops from the heads of garlic, with a sharp knife.

2 Put the garlic heads in a small roasting tin or wrap them in foil together with a few sprigs of rosemary, brush with the olive oil and roast for 20-25 minutes, until soft.

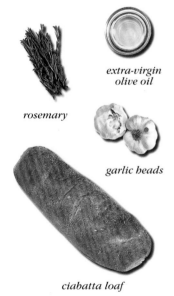

rosemary

extra-virgin olive oil

garlic heads

ciabatta loaf

3 Slice the bread and brush generously with olive oil. Toast the bread under a medium-hot grill until golden, turning once to toast the other side.

4 Squeeze the garlic cloves from their skins on to the toasts. Sprinkle the toasts with chopped fresh rosemary and a little extra olive oil, season and serve.

COOK'S TIP
Roast a few aubergine, pepper or onion slices, to spread over the toasts, for variety.

Stir-fried Spinach with Garlic and Sesame Seeds

The sesame seeds add a crunchy texture which contrasts well with the wilted spinach in this easy vegetable dish.

Serves 2

INGREDIENTS

225 g/8 oz fresh spinach, washed
25 ml/1½ tbsp sesame seeds
30 ml/2 tbsp peanut oil
1.5 ml/¼ tsp sea salt flakes
2-3 garlic cloves, sliced

garlic

spinach

sesame seeds

peanut oil

1 Gently shake the spinach to get rid of any excess water, then cut out the stalks and discard any yellow or damaged leaves. On a chopping board, lay several spinach leaves one on top of another, roll up tightly and cut crossways into wide strips. Repeat with the remaining leaves.

COOK'S TIP

Take care when adding the spinach to the hot oil, as it will spit furiously.

2 Heat a wok to medium heat, add the sesame seeds and dry-fry, stirring, for 1-2 minutes, until the seeds are golden brown. Transfer to a small bowl and set aside.

3 Add the oil to the wok and swirl it around. When hot, add the salt, spinach and garlic and stir-fry for 2 minutes until the spinach just wilts and the leaves are coated with the oil.

4 Sprinkle over the sesame seeds and toss well. Serve at once.

Chicken with Roasted Garlic Cloves

This recipe contains abundant amounts of garlic and the slow cooking makes it soft and fragrant as the delicious flavour permeates the chicken.

Serves 4-6

INGREDIENTS

½ lemon
fresh rosemary sprigs
1.5-1.75 kg/3-4½ lb chicken
4 or 5 heads of garlic
60 ml/4 tbsp olive oil
salt and freshly ground black pepper
steamed broad beans and spring
   onions, to serve

black
pepper

garlic

spring onions

rosemary

lemon

olive oil

broad beans

1 Preheat the oven to 190°C/375°F/ Gas 5. Place the lemon half and the rosemary sprigs in the chicken. Separate 3 or 4 of the garlic heads into cloves and remove the papery husks, but do not peel completely. Slice the top off the other garlic head.

2 Heat the oil in a large flameproof casserole. Add the chicken, turning it in the hot oil to coat the skin completely. Season and add all the garlic.

3 Cover the casserole with a sheet of foil, then the lid, to seal in the steam and the flavour. Cook for 1-1¼ hours until the chicken is cooked. Serve the chicken with the garlic, accompanied by steamed broad beans and spring onions.

COOK'S TIP
Make sure that each guest receives an equal portion of roasted garlic. The idea is to roughly mash the garlic into the pan juices to make an aromatic sauce.

Feta, Roasted Garlic and Oregano Pizza

This pizza is ideal for garlic lovers! Mash down the cloves as you eat – they should be soft and will have lost their pungency.

Serves 4

INGREDIENTS

1 x 150 g/5 oz packet pizza base mix
120 ml/4 fl oz/½ cup lukewarm
    water
1 medium garlic bulb, split into
    cloves
45 ml/3 tbsp olive oil
1 medium red pepper, quartered
    and seeded
1 medium yellow pepper, quartered
    and seeded
2 plum tomatoes
175 g/6 oz feta, crumbled
15-30 ml/1-2 tbsp chopped fresh
    oregano, to garnish

feta

plum tomatoes

olive oil

garlic

peppers

oregano

1 Empty the contents of the pizza base packet into a bowl, then pour in the water and mix to a dough. Turn on to a lightly floured surface and knead for 5 minutes until smooth. Set aside.

2 Preheat the oven to 220°C/425°F / Gas 7. Toss the garlic cloves in 15 ml/ 1 tbsp of the oil. Place the peppers skin-side up on a baking sheet and grill until the skins are charred. After 10 minutes, peel off the skins. Cut the flesh into strips.

3 Put the tomatoes in a bowl and pour over boiling water. Leave for 30 seconds, then plunge into cold water. Peel, seed and roughly chop the flesh. Divide the dough into 4 pieces, then roll out each one to a 13 cm/5 in circle.

4 Place the dough on greased baking sheets. Brush with half the remaining oil and scatter over the tomatoes. Top with the peppers, feta and garlic. Drizzle over the remaining oil. Bake for 15-20 minutes until crisp. Garnish and serve.

Hungarian Beef Goulash

Goulash is Hungary's most famous dish, and paprika is an essential ingredient.

Serves 4

INGREDIENTS

30 ml/2 tbsp vegetable oil
1 kg/2¼ lb braising steak, cubed
2 onions, chopped
1 garlic clove, crushed
15 ml/1 tbsp plain flour
10 ml/2 tsp paprika
5 ml/1 tsp caraway seeds
400 g/14 oz can chopped tomatoes
300 ml/½ pint/1¼ cups beef stock
1 large carrot, chopped
1 red pepper, seeded and chopped
soured cream and paprika, to
    garnish

FOR THE DUMPLINGS

115 g/4 oz self-raising flour
50 g/2 oz shredded suet
15 ml/1 tbsp chopped fresh parsley
2.5 ml/½ tsp caraway seeds
salt and freshly ground black pepper

chopped tomatoes
vegetable oil
garlic
red pepper
beef stock
carrot
pepper
caraway seeds
paprika
onions
flour
soured cream
parsley

1 Heat the oil in a flameproof casserole, add the meat and fry over a high heat for 5 minutes, stirring, until browned. Remove with a slotted spoon.

2 Add the onions and garlic and fry gently for 5 minutes, until softened. Add the flour, paprika and caraway seeds, stir and cook for 3 minutes. Return the browned meat to the casserole and stir in the tomatoes and stock. Bring to the boil, cover and simmer gently for 2 hours.

3 Meanwhile, make the dumplings. Sift the flour and seasoning into a bowl. Add the suet, chopped parsley, caraway seeds and about 45-60 ml/3-4 tbsp cold water and mix to a soft dough. Divide into 8 pieces and roll into balls. Cover and reserve.

4 After 2 hours, stir the carrot and pepper into the goulash and season well. Arrange the dumplings carefully on top of the goulash, cover and simmer for about 25 minutes. Serve in bowls topped with a spoonful of soured cream and sprinkled with a pinch of paprika.

Paprika Pork with Fennel and Caraway

Fennel always tastes very good with pork, and combined with caraway seeds adds an aromatic flavour to this Middle European dish.

Serves 4

INGREDIENTS

15 ml/1 tbsp olive oil
4 boneless pork steaks
1 large onion, thickly sliced
400 g/14 oz can chopped tomatoes
5 ml/1 tsp fennel seeds, lightly
    crushed
2.5 ml/½ tsp caraway seeds, lightly
    crushed
15 ml/1 tbsp paprika
30 ml/2 tbsp soured cream
salt and freshly ground black pepper
paprika, to garnish
buttered noodles and poppy seeds,
    to serve

1 Heat the oil in a large frying pan. Add the pork steaks and brown on both sides. Lift out the steaks and put them on a plate.

paprika

black pepper

tomatoes

salt

fennel seeds

noodles

pork steaks

poppy seeds

onion

soured cream

2 Add the onion to the oil remaining in the pan. Cook for 10 minutes, until soft and golden. Stir in the tomatoes, fennel, caraway seeds and paprika.

3 Return the pork to the pan and simmer gently for 20-30 minutes until tender. Season with salt and pepper. Lightly swirl in the soured cream and sprinkle with a little paprika. Serve with noodles tossed in butter and sprinkled with poppy seeds.

COOK'S TIP
Always buy good quality paprika and store it in a cool dark place as it loses its distinctive flavour very quickly.

Blackened Paprika Redfish

Be brave about heating the pan over a high flame.
As it heats it will develop a smoky patina, which
shows it is then ready for cooking the fish.

Serves 2

INGREDIENTS

2 fillets of redfish, not less than
    2 cm/¾ in thick
75 g/3 oz butter
5 ml/1 tsp paprika
2.5 ml/½ tsp dried oregano
1.5 ml/¼ tsp salt
good pinch each of garlic salt and
    cayenne
good grinding of black pepper
lime slices or lemon wedges, to
    garnish
mixed salad, to serve

salt *butter* *paprika* *black pepper* *garlic salt* *redfish* *cayenne* *oregano*

1 Ensure that the fillets are thawed if frozen. Pat dry with kitchen paper.

3 Place a heavy frying pan over a medium-high heat and heat for 5 minutes. It will smoke and develop a grey-white patina.

2 Melt the butter and swirl in all the seasonings. Pour over the fish and turn the fish in the butter to keep it coated on both sides until you are ready to cook.

4 Turn the fillets once more in the butter and place skin-side down in the pan. Cook, pressing down with a fish slice, for 2 minutes or until the skin is crisp and very dark, but not burnt.

5 Pour a little of the seasoned butter over the top of each fillet and turn them over. Cook for a further 2 minutes or so, again pressing down with a fish slice. Arrange on two warmed serving plates and pour over the seasoned butter. Garnish with lime slices or lemon wedges and serve with a mixed salad.

COOK'S TIP

If you can't get hold of any fresh or frozen redfish fillets, you can substitute it with fillets of fresh or frozen white sea bass. The spiced butter is also delicious with chicken breasts.

Prawn Creole

This spicy prawn dish is very popular in New Orleans, Louisiana. This is an updated, more *"haute Creole"* version.

Serves 6-8

INGREDIENTS

75 g/3 oz unsalted butter
1 large onion, halved and thinly sliced
1 large green pepper, halved, seeded and thinly sliced
2 celery sticks, thinly sliced
2 garlic cloves, thinly sliced
1 bay leaf
30 ml/2 tbsp paprika
450 g/1 lb tomatoes, peeled and chopped
250 ml/8 fl oz/1 cup tomato juice
20 ml/4 tsp Worcestershire sauce
4-6 dashes Tabasco sauce
7.5 ml/1½ tsp cornflour
1.5 kg/3 lb raw prawns, peeled and de-veined
salt
chopped fresh parsley and grated lemon peel, to garnish
boiled rice, to serve

butter
tomatoes
garlic
onion
parsley
bay leaf
lemon peel
green pepper
Tabasco sauce
paprika
celery
prawns
tomato juice

1 Melt 25 g/1 oz of the butter in a large pan and sauté the onion, green pepper, celery, garlic and bay leaf for 1-2 minutes until all are hot and coated in butter.

2 Add the paprika, tomatoes and tomato juice, stir in the Worcestershire and Tabasco sauces, bring to the boil and simmer, uncovered, until reduced by about a quarter, and vegetables are soft.

3 Blend the cornflour with 75 ml/ 5 tbsp cold water and pour it into the tomato sauce. Stir the sauce continuously over the heat for a couple of minutes, then turn off the heat.

4 Sauté the prawns in batches in the remaining butter for 2-4 minutes, until they are pink and tender.

5 Meanwhile, reheat the tomato sauce. When all the prawns are cooked, add them to the sauce and stir over the heat for no more than 1 minute. Adjust the seasoning and serve with boiled rice, garnished with chopped fresh parsley and grated lemon peel.

COOK'S TIP

Pre-cooked prawns may be all that are available, in which case incorporate all the butter into the sauce-making, skip the sauté stage and add the ready-cooked prawns to the sauce when reheating it, giving them just long enough to heat through.

Saffron Pappardelle

Saffron gives this delicate dish a pretty colour and exquisite flavour. Serve for a summer lunch or as a light supper.

Serves 4

INGREDIENTS

large pinch of saffron strands
4 sun-dried tomatoes, chopped
5 ml/1 tsp fresh thyme
12 large cooked prawns in their
    shells
225 g/8 oz baby squid
225 g/8 oz monkfish fillet
2-3 garlic cloves, crushed
2 small onions, quartered
1 small bulb fennel, trimmed and
    sliced
150 ml/¼ pint/⅔ cup white wine
225 g/8 oz pappardelle
salt
30 ml/2 tbsp chopped fresh parsley,
    to garnish

saffron strands

fennel

baby squid

pappardelle

sun-dried tomatoes

parsley

monkfish fillet

thyme

onion

prawns

white wine

1 Put the saffron, sun-dried tomatoes and thyme into a bowl with 60 ml/4 tbsp hot water. Leave to soak for 30 minutes.

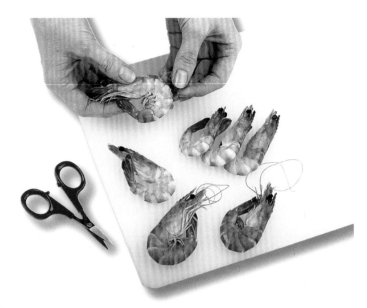

2 Wash the prawns and carefully remove the shells, leaving the heads and tails intact. Pull the head from the body of each squid and remove the quill. Cut the tentacles from the head and rinse under cold water. Pull off the outer skin and cut the flesh into 5 mm/¼ in rings. Cut the monkfish into 2.5 cm/1 in cubes.

3 Put the garlic, onions and fennel into a pan with the wine. Cover and simmer for 5 minutes until tender.

4 Add the monkfish, saffron, tomatoes and thyme in their liquid. Cover and cook for 3 minutes. Then add the prawns and squid. Cover and cook gently for 1-2 minutes (do not overcook or the squid will become tough).

5 Meanwhile cook the pasta in a large pan of boiling, salted water until al dente. Drain thoroughly.

70

VARIATION

You can try any kind of shaped pasta for this recipe. Farfalle or conchiglie will hold the sauce and look attractive too.

6 Divide the pasta among 4 serving dishes and top with the fish and shellfish sauce. Sprinkle with parsley and serve at once.

Pumpkin and Pistachio Risotto with Saffron

This elegant combination of creamy golden rice and orange pumpkin can be as pale or bright as you like depending on the amount of saffron used.

Serves 4

INGREDIENTS

1.1 litres/2 pints/5 cups vegetable stock or water
generous pinch of saffron threads
30 ml/2 tbsp olive oil
1 medium onion, chopped
2 garlic cloves, crushed
450 g/1 lb arborio rice
900 g/2 lb pumpkin, peeled, seeded and cut into 2 cm/$^{3}\!/_{4}$ in cubes
250 ml/8 fl oz/1 cup dry white wine
15 g/$^{1}\!/_{2}$ oz Parmesan cheese, finely grated
50 g/2 oz pistachios
45 ml/3 tbsp chopped fresh marjoram or oregano, plus extra leaves to garnish
salt, freshly grated nutmeg and ground black pepper

pistachios *Parmesan* *white wine*

garlic *marjoram* *saffron*

arborio rice *pumpkin*

onion

1 Bring the stock or water to the boil and reduce to a low simmer. Ladle a little stock into a small bowl. Add the saffron threads and leave to infuse.

2 Heat the oil in a large saucepan. Add the onion and garlic and cook gently for about 5 minutes until softened. Add the rice and cubed pumpkin and cook for a few more minutes until the rice looks transparent.

3 Pour in the white wine, turn up the heat and allow it to bubble hard. When it is absorbed add one quarter of the stock together with the infused saffron and liquid. Stir constantly until all the liquid is absorbed.

4 Continue to add the stock or water, a ladleful at a time, allowing the rice to absorb the liquid before adding more and stirring all the time. After 20-30 minutes the rice should be golden yellow and al dente when tested.

5 Stir in the Parmesan cheese, cover the pan and leave to stand for 5 minutes.

6 Just before serving, stir in the pistachios and marjoram or oregano. Season to taste with salt, freshly grated nutmeg and pepper, and then scatter over a few extra fresh marjoram or oregano leaves.

Onion Bhajias

Bhajias are a classic snack of India. The same batter may be used with a variety of vegetables.

Makes 20-25

INGREDIENTS

225 g/8 oz gram flour
2.5 ml/½ tsp chilli powder
5 ml/1 tsp ground turmeric
5 ml/1 tsp baking powder
1.5 ml/¼ tsp asafoetida
2.5 ml/½ tsp each nigella, fennel, cumin and onion seeds, coarsely crushed
2 large onions, finely sliced
2 green chillies, seeded and finely chopped
50 g/2 oz fresh coriander leaves, chopped
salt, to taste
vegetable oil, for deep-frying

green chillies

coriander

salt

vegetable oil

baking powder

water   chilli powder

nigella, fennel, cumin and onion seeds   gram flour

onions   ground turmeric   asafoetida

1 In a bowl, mix together the flour, chilli, turmeric, baking powder, asafoetida and salt to taste and then sift into a large mixing bowl.

2 Add the nigella, fennel, cumin and onion seeds, together with the onions, chillies and coriander leaves and toss together well. Very gradually mix in enough cold water to make a stiff, thick batter.

3 Heat enough oil in a karahi or wok for deep-frying. Carefully place spoonfuls of the mixture in the hot oil and fry until they are golden brown. Leave sufficient space to turn the fritters. Drain well and serve immediately.

Oranges with Saffron Yogurt

This is a popular Indian dessert after a hot and spicy curry.

Serves 4

INGREDIENTS

4 large oranges
1.25 ml/¼ tsp ground cinnamon
150 ml/¼ pint/⅔ cup natural yogurt
10 ml/2 tsp caster sugar
3-4 saffron strands
1.5 ml/¼ tsp ground ginger
15 ml/1 tbsp chopped pistachio
    nuts, toasted
fresh lemon balm or mint leaves,
    to decorate

yogurt

saffron strands

caster sugar

mint leaves

pistachio nuts

oranges

ground cinnamon

ground ginger

1 Slice the bottom off each of the oranges. Working from the top of the orange, cut across the top of the orange and down one side. Follow the contours of the orange. Repeat until all the peel and pith has been removed, reserving any juice. Peel the remaining oranges in the same way.

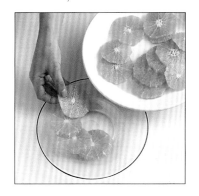

2 Slice the oranges thinly and remove any pips. Lay in a single layer, overlapping the slices, on a shallow serving platter. Sprinkle the ground cinnamon over the oranges. Cover the platter with clear film and chill.

3 Mix the yogurt, sugar, saffron and ginger together in a bowl and leave to infuse for 5–10 minutes. Sprinkle with the chopped nuts. To serve, spoon the yogurt and nut mixture over the chilled orange slices.

COOK'S TIP

For a more unusual dessert use deliciously juicy blood oranges, which look dramatic and have a wonderful flavour.

Harissa-spiced Chicken

The spices and fruit in this stuffing give the chicken a good flavour and help to keep it moist.

Serves 4-5

INGREDIENTS

1.5 kg/3-3½ lb chicken
30-60 ml/2-4 tbsp garlic and spice oil
a few bay leaves
10 ml/2 tsp clear honey
10 ml/2 tsp tomato purée
60 ml/4 tbsp lemon juice
150 ml/¼ pint/⅔ cup chicken stock
2.5-5ml/½-1 tsp harissa

FOR THE STUFFING

25 g/1 oz/2 tbsp butter
1 onion, chopped
1 garlic clove, crushed
7.5 ml/1½ tsp ground cinnamon
2.5 ml/½ tsp ground cumin
225 g/8 oz dried fruit, soaked for several hours or overnight in water to cover
25 g/1 oz blanched almonds, finely chopped
salt and freshly ground black pepper

1 Make the stuffing. Melt the butter in a saucepan, add the onion and garlic and cook gently for 5 minutes until soft. Add the ground cinnamon and cumin and cook, stirring, for 2 minutes.

2 Drain the dried fruit, chop it roughly and add to the stuffing with the almonds. Season with salt and pepper and cook for 2 minutes more. Spoon into a bowl and leave to cool.

pepper
garlic
dried fruit
water
ground cumin
blanched almonds
onion
bay leaves
lemon juice
salt
chicken
butter
tomato purée
chicken stock
ground cinnamon
clear honey
garlic and spice oil

3 Preheat the oven to 200°C/400°F/ Gas 6. Stuff the neck of the chicken with the fruit mixture, reserving any excess. Brush the garlic and spice oil over the chicken. Place the chicken in a roasting tin, tuck in the bay leaves and roast for 1-1¼ hours, basting occasionally with the juices, until cooked.

4 Transfer the chicken to a carving board. Pour off any excess fat from the roasting tin. Stir the honey, tomato purée, lemon juice, stock and harissa into the juices in the tin and add salt to taste. Bring to the boil, then simmer for 2 minutes, stirring frequently. Meanwhile, reheat any extra stuffing. Carve the chicken, pour the sauce into a bowl, and serve with the stuffing and chicken.

Duck with Harissa

Harissa, mixed with cinnamon, saffron and preserved lemon, gives this colourful casserole an unforgettable flavour.

Serves 4

INGREDIENTS

15 ml/1 tbsp olive oil
1.75 kg/4-4½ lb duck, quartered
1 large onion, thinly sliced
1 garlic clove, crushed
2.5 ml/½ tsp ground cumin
400 ml/14 fl oz/1¾ cups duck or
    chicken stock
juice of ½ lemon
5-10 ml/1-2 tsp harissa
1 cinnamon stick
5ml/1 tsp saffron strands
50 g/2 oz black olives
50 g/2 oz green olives
1 preserved lemon, rinsed, drained
    and cut into fine strips
2-3 lemon slices
30 ml/2 tbsp chopped fresh
    coriander
salt and freshly ground black pepper
coriander sprigs, to garnish

1 Heat the oil in a flameproof casserole and fry the duck quarters until browned all over. Remove with a slotted spoon and set aside. Add the onion and garlic to the casserole and cook for 5 minutes until soft, then add the ground cumin and cook, for 2 minutes, stirring all the time.

onion

garlic

cinnamon stick

olive oil

salt

lemon juice

ground cumin

saffron strands

lemon slices

duck or chicken stock

duck

green and black olives

fresh coriander

2 Pour in the stock and lemon juice, then add the harissa, cinnamon and saffron. Bring to the boil. Return the duck to the casserole and add the olives, preserved lemon peel and lemon slices. Season with salt and pepper.

3 Reduce the heat, partially cover the casserole and simmer gently for 45 minutes until the duck is cooked through. Discard the cinnamon stick. Stir in the chopped coriander and garnish with the coriander sprigs.

Hot and Sour Pork

Chinese five-spice powder is made from a mixture of ground star anise, Szechuan pepper, cassia or cinnamon, cloves and fennel seeds and has a flavour similar to liquorice.

Serves 4

INGREDIENTS

350 g/12 oz pork fillet
5 ml/1 tsp sunflower oil
2.5 cm/1 in piece fresh root ginger, grated
1 red chilli, seeded and finely chopped
5 ml/1 tsp Chinese five-spice powder
15 ml/1 tbsp sherry vinegar
15 ml/1 tbsp soy sauce
225 g/8 oz can pineapple chunks in natural juice
175 ml/6 fl oz/¾ cup chicken stock
20 ml/4 tsp cornflour
1 small green pepper, seeded and sliced
115 g/4 oz baby sweetcorn, halved
salt and freshly ground black pepper
sprig of flat-leaf parsley, to garnish
boiled rice to serve

chicken stock

five-spice powder

ginger

pork fillet

pepper

sherry vinegar

cornflour

baby sweetcorn   chilli   pineapple chunks   soy sauce

1 Pre-heat the oven to 160°C/325°F/ Gas 3. Trim away any fat from the pork and cut into 1 cm/½ in thick slices.

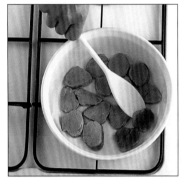

2 Brush the oil over the base of a large flameproof casserole. Heat over a medium flame and then fry the meat for about 2 minutes on each side or until the meat is lightly browned.

3 Blend together the ginger, chilli, five-spice powder, vinegar and soy sauce.

4 Drain the pineapple chunks, reserving the juice. Make the stock up to 300 ml/½ pint/1¼ cups with the reserved juice, mix together with the spices and pour over the pork.

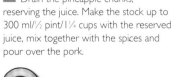

5 Slowly bring to the boil. Blend the cornflour with 15ml/1tbsp of cold water and gradually stir into the pork. Add the vegetables and season to taste.

6 Cover and cook in the oven for 30 minutes. Stir in the pineapple and cook for a further 5 minutes. Garnish with flat-leaf parsley and serve with boiled rice.

Stir-fried Five-spice Squid with Black Bean Sauce

Squid is perfect for stir-frying as it should be cooked quickly. The spicy sauce makes the ideal accompaniment.

Serves 6

INGREDIENTS

450 g/1 lb small cleaned squid
45 ml/3 tbsp oil
2.5 cm/1 in piece fresh root ginger, grated
1 garlic clove, crushed
8 spring onions, cut diagonally into 2.5 cm/1 in lengths
1 red pepper, seeded and cut into strips
1 fresh green chilli, seeded and thinly sliced
6 mushrooms, sliced
5 ml/1 tsp five-spice powder
30 ml/2 tbsp black bean sauce
30 ml/2 tbsp soy sauce
5 ml/1 tsp granulated sugar
15 ml/1 tbsp rice wine or dry sherry

1 Rinse the squid and pull away the outer skin. Dry on kitchen paper. Using a sharp knife, slit the squid open and score the outside of the flesh into diamonds with a sharp knife. Cut the squid into strips.

green chilli granulated sugar oil
mushrooms fresh root ginger
garlic spring onions
squid five-spice powder red pepper
soy sauce black bean sauce dry sherry
rice wine

COOK'S TIP

As with all stir-fried dishes, it is important to have every ingredient cut or prepared before you start to cook.

2 Heat the wok briefly and add the oil. When it is hot, stir-fry the squid for 2-3 minutes then transfer to a plate with a slotted spoon. Add the ginger, garlic, spring onions, red pepper, chilli and mushrooms and stir-fry for 2 minutes.

3 Return the squid to the wok and stir in the five-spice powder together with the black bean sauce, soy sauce, sugar and rice wine or sherry. Bring to the boil and cook, stirring, for 1 minute. Serve at once.

Hot Spicy Crab Claws

Crab claws are stir-fried in a delicious spicy sauce in this quick appetizer based on an Indonesian dish called Kepiting Pedas.

Serves 4

INGREDIENTS

12 fresh or frozen and thawed
    cooked crab claws
4 shallots, coarsely chopped
2-4 fresh red chillies, seeded and
    coarsely chopped
3 garlic cloves, coarsely chopped
5 ml/1 tsp grated fresh root ginger
2.5 ml/½ tsp ground coriander
45 ml/3 tbsp peanut oil
10 ml/2 tsp sweet soy sauce
10-15 ml/2-3 tsp lime juice
salt
fresh coriander sprigs, to garnish

crab claws

peanut oil

coriander

shallots

red chillies

garlic

sweet soy sauce

lime

ginger

1 Crack the crab claws with the back of a heavy knife to make eating easier. Set aside. In a mortar, pound the chopped shallots with the pestle until pulpy. Add the chillies, garlic, ginger and ground coriander and pound until the mixture forms a coarse paste.

2 Heat the wok over a medium heat, add the oil and swirl it around. When it is hot, add in the chilli paste and stir-fry for about 30 seconds. Increase the heat to high and add the crab claws. Stir-fry for another 3-4 minutes.

3 Add the sweet soy sauce, lime juice, 60ml/4 tbsp water and salt to taste. Continue to stir-fry for 1-2 minutes then serve, garnished with fresh coriander. The crab claws are eaten with the fingers, so provide finger bowls.

COOK'S TIP
If whole crab claws are unavailable, look out for frozen prepared crab claws. These are shelled with just the tip of the claw attached to the white meat. Stir-fry for about 2 minutes until heated through.

Chicken Jalfrezi

This is a stir-fried dish cooked with onions, ginger and garlic in a rich pepper sauce.

Serves 4

INGREDIENTS

675 g/1½ lb chicken breasts, skinned
30 ml/2 tbsp vegetable oil
5 ml/1 tsp cumin seeds
1 onion, finely chopped
1 green pepper, seeded and finely chopped
1 red pepper, seeded and finely chopped
1 garlic clove, crushed
2 cm/¾ in piece fresh root ginger, finely chopped
15 ml/1 tbsp curry paste
1.5 ml/¼ tsp chilli powder
5 ml/1 tsp ground coriander
5 ml/1 tsp ground cumin
2.5 ml/½ tsp salt
400 g/14 oz can chopped tomatoes
30 ml/2 tbsp chopped fresh coriander
fresh coriander sprigs, to garnish
boiled rice, to serve

onion, ginger, garlic, fresh coriander, peppers, chicken, chopped tomatoes, chilli powder, curry paste, ground cumin, oil, ground coriander, cumin seeds, salt

1 Discard any fat or skin from the chicken and cut into 2.5 cm/1 in cubes.

2 Heat the oil in a wok and fry the cumin seeds for 2 minutes until they splutter. Add the onion, peppers, garlic and ginger and stir-fry for 6-8 minutes.

3 Add the curry paste and fry for about 2 minutes. Stir in the chilli powder, ground coriander, cumin and salt and 15 ml/1 tbsp water. Stir well and cook for a further 2 minutes.

4 Add the chicken and cook for about 5 minutes, then add the tomatoes and coriander. Cover and cook for about 15 minutes or until the chicken is tender. Serve with rice; garnished with coriander.

Spicy Potatoes and Cauliflower

This dish is simplicity itself to make and may be eaten as a vegetarian main meal for two with Indian breads or rice, a raita, such as cucumber and yogurt, and a fresh mint relish.

Serves 2

INGREDIENTS

200 g/8 oz potatoes
75 ml/5 tbsp peanut oil
5 ml/1 tsp ground cumin
5 ml/1 tsp ground coriander
1.5 ml/¼ tsp ground turmeric
1.5 ml/¼ tsp cayenne pepper
1 green chilli, seeded and finely chopped
1 medium cauliflower, broken into small florets
5 ml/1 tsp cumin seeds
2 garlic cloves, cut into shreds
15-30 ml/1-2 tbsp finely chopped fresh coriander
salt

coriander   cauliflower

potatoes   cumin seeds   turmeric

cayenne pepper

garlic

green chilli

1 Boil the potatoes in their skins in boiling, salted water for about 20 minutes until just tender. Drain and let cool. When cool enough to handle, peel and cut into 2.5 cm/1 in cubes.

2 Heat 45ml/3 tbsp of the oil in a wok or kahari. When hot, add the ground cumin, coriander, turmeric, and cayenne pepper together with the chilli. Let the spices sizzle for a few seconds.

3 Add the cauliflower and about 60ml/4 tbsp water. Cook, stirring continuously, for 6-8 minutes over medium heat. Add the potatoes and stir-fry for 2-3 minutes. Season to taste, then remove from the heat.

4 Heat the remaining oil in a small frying pan. When hot, add the cumin seeds and garlic and cook until lightly browned. Pour the mixture over the vegetables. Sprinkle with the chopped coriander and serve at once.

Cinnamon and Green Peppercorn Crusted Lamb

Racks of lamb are ideal for serving at dinner parties. This version has a spiced crumb coating.

Serves 6

INGREDIENTS

50 g/2 oz ciabatta bread
15 ml/1 tbsp drained green
 peppercorns in brine, lightly
 crushed
15 ml/1 tbsp ground cinnamon
1 garlic clove, crushed
2.5 ml/½ tsp salt
25 g/1 oz butter, melted
10ml/2 tsp Dijon mustard
2 racks of lamb, trimmed
60 ml/4 tbsp red wine
400 ml/14 fl oz/1⅔ cups lamb stock
15 ml/1 tbsp balsamic vinegar
fresh vegetables, to serve

1 Preheat the oven to 220°C/425°F/ Gas 7. Break the ciabatta into pieces, spread out on a baking sheet and bake for 10 minutes or until pale golden. Process in a blender or food processor to make crumbs.

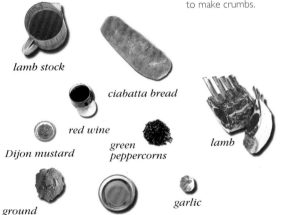

lamb stock

ciabatta bread

red wine

Dijon mustard

green peppercorns

lamb

ground cinnamon

balsamic vinegar

garlic

VARIATION
The spicy crumbs also make a tasty coating for chicken pieces, fish or chops.

2 Tip the crumbs into a bowl, add the green peppercorns, cinnamon, garlic and salt and then stir in the melted butter. Spread the mustard over the lamb and press the crumb mixture on to the mustard to make a thin even crust. Put the racks in a roasting tin and roast for 30 minutes, covering the ends with foil if they start to over-brown.

3 Remove the lamb to a carving dish and keep hot under tented foil. Skim the fat off the juices in the roasting tin. Stir in the wine, stock and vinegar. Bring to the boil, stirring in any sediment, then lower the heat and simmer for about 10 minutes until reduced to a rich gravy. Carve the lamb and serve with the gravy and a selection of fresh vegetables.

Chicken Couscous

A spicy dish with more than a hint of warming Middle-eastern spices.

Serves 4

INGREDIENTS

15 ml/1 tbsp butter
15 ml/1 tbsp sunflower oil
4 chicken portions
2 onions, finely chopped
2 garlic cloves, crushed
2.5ml/½ tsp ground cinnamon
1.25ml/¼ tsp ground ginger
1.25ml/¼ tsp ground turmeric
30ml/2 tbsp orange juice
10ml/2 tsp clear honey
salt
fresh mint sprigs, to garnish

FOR THE COUSCOUS

350 g/12 oz/2¼ cups couscous
5 ml/1 tsp salt
10 ml/2 tsp caster sugar
30 ml/2 tbsp sunflower oil
2.5ml/½ tsp ground cinnamon
pinch of grated nutmeg
15 ml/1 tbsp orange blossom water
30 ml/2 tbsp sultanas
50 g/2 oz/½ cup blanched almonds,
    chopped
45 ml/3 tbsp pistachio nuts,
    chopped

nutmeg ground turmeric
sultanas
cinnamon orange blossom water
mint grouna ginger
orange juice
honey couscous pistachio nuts blanched almonds chicken ground cinnamon

1 Heat the butter and oil in a large pan and add the chicken portions, skin side down. Fry for 3-4 minutes, until the skin is golden, then turn over.

2 Add the onions, garlic, spices and a pinch of salt and pour over the orange juice mixed with 300ml/½ pint/1¼ cups of water. Cover and bring to the boil, then reduce the heat and simmer for about 30 minutes.

3 Meanwhile, cover the couscous and salt with 350 ml/12 fl oz/1½ cups water. Stir once and leave to stand for 5 minutes. Add the caster sugar, 15 ml/ 1 tbsp of the oil, the cinnamon, nutmeg, orange blossom water and sultanas and mix well. Heat the remaining oil in a pan and fry the almonds until golden. Stir into the couscous with the pistachio nuts.

4 Line a steamer with greaseproof paper and spoon in the couscous. Place the steamer over the chicken and steam for 10 minutes. Then remove and keep covered. Stir the honey into the chicken liquid and boil rapidly for 3-4 minutes. Spoon the couscous on to a platter and top with the chicken, with a little sauce spooned over. Garnish with mint and serve with the remaining sauce.

Lentils and Rice with Cloves

Lentils are cooked with whole and ground spices, potatoes, rice and onions to produce a delicious Indian-style risotto.

Serves 4

INGREDIENTS

150 g/5 oz toovar dhal or red split
   lentils
115 g/4 oz basmati rice
1 large potato
1 large onion
30 ml/2 tbsp vegetable oil
7 whole cloves
1.5 ml/¼ tsp cumin seeds
1.5 ml/¼ tsp ground turmeric
10 ml/2 tsp salt

basmati rice

cumin seeds

ground turmeric

cloves

salt

red split lentils

potato

onion

vegetable oil

1 Wash the toovar dhal or lentils and rice in several changes of cold water. Place in a bowl and cover with water. Leave to soak for 15 minutes, then drain.

2 Cut the potato into 2.5 cm/1 in chunks, and rinse thoroughly under cold running water to remove any excess starch.

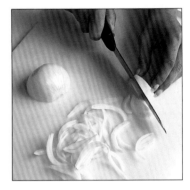

3 Using a sharp knife, cut the onion into thin slices.

4 Heat the oil in a large heavy-based saucepan and fry the cloves and cumin seeds for 2 minutes until the seeds are beginning to splutter.

5 Add the onion and potatoes and fry for 5 minutes, then add the lentils, rice, turmeric and salt and fry for 3 minutes.

6 Add 300ml/½ pint/1¼ cups water. Bring to the boil, cover and simmer for 15–20 minutes until all the water has been absorbed and the potatoes are tender. Leave to stand, covered, for 10 minutes before serving.

Spiced Bread Pudding with Cranberry Sauce

Nutmeg is a warm, aromatic spice and is particularly suited to old-fashioned puddings.

Serves 6-8

INGREDIENTS

50 g/2 oz butter, melted
750 ml/1¼ pints/3 cups milk
3 eggs
90 g/3½ oz caster sugar
5 ml/1 tsp vanilla essence
10 ml/2 tsp ground cinnamon
2.5 ml/½ tsp grated nutmeg
400 g/14 oz cubed bread cut from
    a day-old French loaf
50 g/2 oz chopped walnut kernels
75 g/3 oz sultanas

FOR THE CRANBERRY SAUCE

350 g/12 oz cranberries, fresh or
    frozen
finely grated peel and juice of
    1 large orange
25 g/1 oz caster sugar

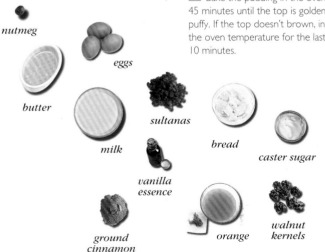

nutmeg

eggs

butter

sultanas

milk

bread

caster sugar

vanilla essence

ground cinnamon

orange

walnut kernels

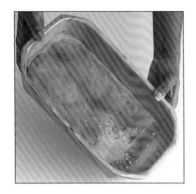

1 Brush the butter generously into the bottom and sides of a medium-sized ovenproof dish. Pour any remaining butter into the milk. Beat the eggs until light and frothy, then beat in the sugar, vanilla essence, cinnamon and nutmeg. Stir in the milk and mix well.

4 Bake the pudding in the oven for 45 minutes until the top is golden and puffy. If the top doesn't brown, increase the oven temperature for the last 10 minutes.

2 Arrange the bread cubes in the prepared dish, scattering the walnuts and sultanas over the top.

3 Preheat the oven to 180°C/350°F/ Gas 4. Pour the custard over the bread, coating each piece thoroughly. Leave to stand for 45 minutes.

5 To make the cranberry sauce, put the berries into a saucepan with the orange peel and juice and the sugar.

6 Stir over a low heat until the sugar dissolves, then cook until the berries pop and the mixture thickens and becomes syrupy. Serve the sauce hot or cold.

Cinnamon Rice Pudding

Cinnamon adds a wonderful flavour to rice pudding. This particular version is from Mexico.

Serves 4

INGREDIENTS

75 g/3 oz raisins
90 g/3½ oz short grain rice
2.5 cm/1 in strip of lime or lemon
    peel
475 ml/16 fl oz/2 cups milk
225 g/8oz granulated sugar
1.5 ml/¼ tsp salt
2.5 cm/1 in cinnamon stick
2 egg yolks, well beaten
15 g/½ oz unsalted butter, cubed
toasted flaked almonds, to decorate
segments of fresh peeled oranges,
    to serve

butter

eggs

granulated sugar

milk

raisins

lime or lemon peel

oranges

short grain rice

cinnamon stick

flaked almonds

1 Put the raisins into a small bowl. Cover with warm water and set aside to soak. Put the short grain rice into a saucepan together with the lime or lemon peel and 250 ml/8 fl oz/1 cup water. Bring slowly to the boil and then lower the heat. Cover the pan and simmer very gently for about 20 minutes or until all the water has been absorbed.

2 Remove the peel from the rice and discard it. Add the milk, sugar, salt and cinnamon stick and cook, stirring, over a very low heat until all the milk has been absorbed. Do not cover the pan. Do not allow to boil.

3 Discard the cinnamon stick. Add the egg yolks and butter, stirring, until the butter has melted and the pudding is rich and creamy. Drain the raisins well and stir them into the rice. Cook the pudding for a few minutes longer.

4 Spoon the rice into a dish and cool. Decorate with flaked almonds and serve with orange segments.

COOK'S TIP

It is essential to use short grain rice for this pudding. This type of rice is sometimes packaged with the name "pudding rice".

Crispy Cinnamon Toasts

This recipe is based on a version of the popular French toast. It is a great favourite for breakfast, especially with children. The Grand Marnier makes this a more adult variation.

Serves 4

INGREDIENTS

50 g/2 oz raisins
45 ml/3 tbsp Grand Marnier
4 medium slices white bread
2–3 eggs, beaten
15 ml/1 tbsp ground cinnamon
2 large oranges
25 ml/1½ tbsp sunflower oil
25 g/1 oz unsalted butter
15 ml/1 tbsp demerara sugar
thick Greek yogurt, to serve

ground cinnamon

orange

raisins

demerara sugar

eggs

sliced white bread

COOK'S TIP
You can use fancy cutters to create a pretty dessert or, if you do not have cutters, simply cut the crusts off the bread and cut it into little fingers.

1 Soak the raisins in the Grand Marnier for 10 minutes or until they plump out nicely.

2 Cut the bread into shapes with a cutter. Place the shapes in a bowl with the eggs and cinnamon to soak.

3 Peel the oranges. Remove any excess pith from the peel, then cut into fine strips and blanch. Refresh the strips in cold water, then drain.

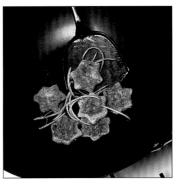

4 Strain the raisins. Heat the wok, then add the oil. When the oil is hot, stir in the butter until melted, then add the bread and fry, turning once, until golden brown. Stir in the raisins and orange rind, and sprinkle with sugar. Serve warm with thick Greek yogurt.

Spiced Chocolate Cake

This cake is flavoured with aromatic cinnamon, cloves, nutmeg and cardamom and makes a perfect end to a meal.

Makes 24

INGREDIENTS

3 eggs
200 g/7 oz caster sugar
115 g/4 oz plain flour
5 ml/1 tsp ground cinnamon
1.5 ml/¼ tsp ground cloves
1.5 ml/¼ tsp freshly grated nutmeg
1.5 ml/¼ tsp ground cardamom
275 g/10 oz unblanched almonds,
    coarsely ground
25 g/1 oz candied lemon peel, finely
    chopped
25 g/1 oz candied orange peel,
    finely chopped
40 g/1½ oz plain chocolate, grated
2.5 ml/½ tsp grated lemon rind
2.5 ml/½ tsp grated orange rind
10 ml/2 tsp rosewater

FOR THE ICING

1 egg white
10 ml/2 tsp cocoa powder, mixed
    with 15 ml/1 tbsp boiling water
    and cooled
115 g/4 oz icing sugar
15 ml/2 tbsp sugar crystals

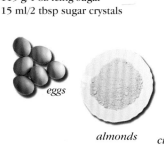
almonds

nutmeg
cloves
chocolate
rose water
candied peel
cinnamon
orange rind
lemon rind

eggs

COOK'S TIP

Do not worry when the top of the cake cracks when you cut it; it is meant to be like that!

1 Preheat the oven to 160°C/325°F/ Gas 3. Line a 30 × 23 cm/12 × 9 in Swiss roll tin with rice paper.

2 Whisk the eggs and caster sugar in a large bowl until thick and pale. Sift in the flour, cinnamon, ground cloves, nutmeg and cardamom and then stir in all the remaining dry ingredients.

3 Spoon evenly into the prepared tin and brush with the rosewater. Bake for 30-35 minutes until firm. Turn out of the tin.

4 To make the icing, stir the egg white into the cocoa mixture, sift in the icing sugar and mix. Spread over the cake while still warm. Sprinkle with sugar crystals and then return to the oven for 5 minutes. Cut into squares when cold.

American Spiced Pumpkin Pie

Pumpkin pie is the most popular and traditional of American desserts. Here it is spiced with cinnamon, ginger and allspice.

Serves 4–6

INGREDIENTS

175 g/6 oz plain flour
pinch of salt
75 g/3oz unsalted butter
15 ml/1 tbsp caster sugar
450 g/1lb peeled fresh pumpkin, cubed, or 400g/14 oz canned pumpkin, drained
115 g/4 oz soft light brown sugar
1.5 ml/¼ tsp salt
1.5 ml/¼ tsp ground allspice
2.5 ml/½ tsp ground cinnamon
2.5 ml/½ tsp ground ginger
2 eggs, lightly beaten
120 ml/4fl oz/½ cup double cream
whipped cream, to serve

salt *butter*
whipped cream *brown sugar*

double cream *caster sugar*

ground allspice

ground cinnamon

 ground ginger *eggs* *pumpkin*

1 Place the flour in a bowl with the salt and butter and rub in with your fingertips until the mixture resembles breadcrumbs. Alternatively, process in a food processor. Stir in the sugar and add about 30-40 ml/2-3 tbsp water and mix to a soft dough. Knead the dough lightly on a floured surface then flatten out into a round, wrap in a polythene bag and chill for about 1 hour.

2 Roll out the pastry quite thinly and use to line a 23 cm/9 in pie dish. Trim off any excess pastry and reserve for the decoration. Prick the base with a fork. Preheat the oven to 200°C/400°F /Gas 6 with a baking sheet inside. If you are using raw pumpkin for the pie, steam for 15 minutes until tender, then leave to cool. Purée the pumpkin in a food processor or blender until very smooth.

3 Cut as many leaf shapes as you can from the excess pastry and make vein markings with the back of a knife on each. Brush the edge of the pastry with water and stick the leaves all round the edge. Chill.

4 Combine the pumpkin purée, sugar, salt, spices, eggs and cream and pour into the case. Place on the baking sheet and bake for 15 minutes. Reduce the temperature to 180°C/350°F/Gas 4 and cook for a further 30 minutes, or until the filling is set. Serve with the cream.

INDEX

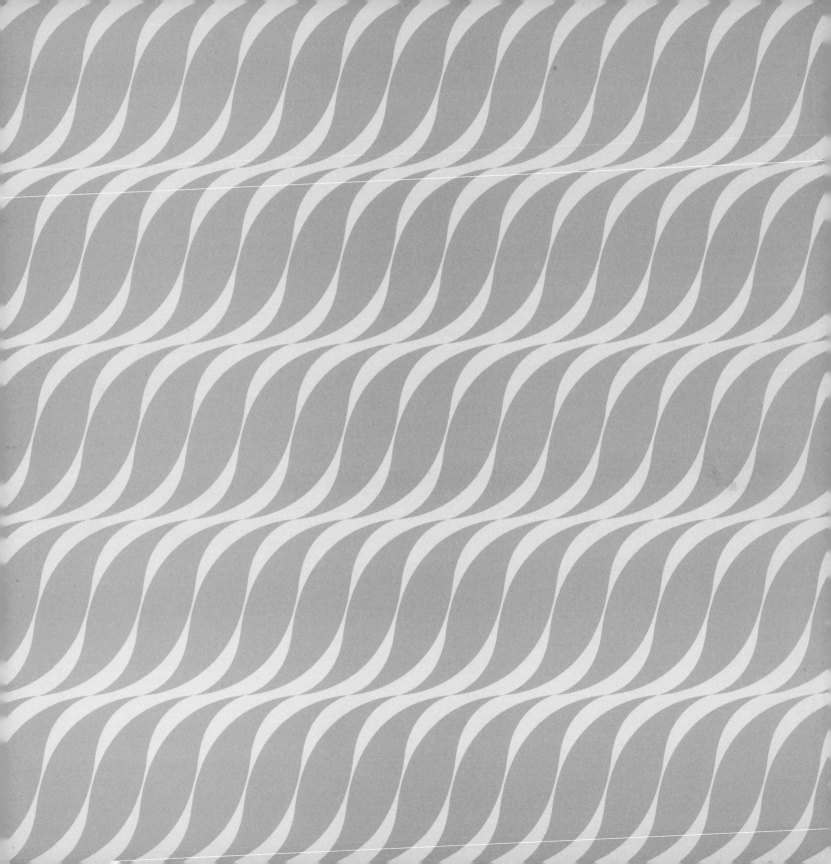